SATURDAY NIGHT AT THE PAHALA THEATRE

LOIS-ANN YAMANAKA

BAMBOO RIDGE PRESS

1993

My deepest gratitude to the following people:

To Faye Kicknosway who believed in a voice long before
the words came and who taught what time looked like
in freeze frame, she said, all played again.

To Eric Chock for teaching.

To Cathy Song for bridges in the work and for honesty.

To Juliet S. Kono for the long talks and
Wing Tek Lum for firm ground.
To the Bamboo Ridge study group for place and reason.
To Darrell H.Y. Lum for the stories in our language.

To Lisa Asagi and Rinehardt Zamora "Zach" Linmark
for *ezra, ezra,* the hours and hours of it, you know what I mean.
To Lori Takayesu and Justin Chin, thank you for the group.

To Sue Cowing and Lee Kyselka in the Women's Study Group,
my thank you for poems on Saturday nights.

And to my husband, John Maurice,
for your love for JohnJohn TSYI and me.

This is a special double issue of *Bamboo Ridge, The Hawaii Writers' Quarterly*, issue numbers 58 and 59, ISSN 0733-0308.

ISBN 0-910043-31-0
Library of Congress Catalog Card Number 93-9139
Indexed in the American Humanities Index
Copyright 1993 Lois-Ann Yamanaka.

Cover art: *"The Birth of Venus"* by Cora Yee. 1992.
Screenprint, goldleaf. 11-1/2" H x 8-1/2" W.
Title page: *"The Mask"* by Cora Yee. 1990.
Screenprint. 1-1/4" x 1-5/8"
Cover and book design: Susanne Yuu
Typesetting: HonBlue Inc.
Printed in the United States.
Published by Bamboo Ridge Press.

Bamboo Ridge is a non-profit, tax exempt organization formed to foster the appreciation, understanding, and creation of literary, visual, audio-visual and performing arts by and about Hawaii's people.
Your tax-deductible contributions are welcomed.
Bamboo Ridge is supported in part by grants from the State Foundation on the Culture and the Arts (SFCA). The SFCA is funded by appropriations from the Hawaii State Legislature and by grants from the National Endowment for the Arts, a federal agency.
Bamboo Ridge Press is a member of the Council of Literary Magazines and Presses (CLMP).

Subscriptions to *Bamboo Ridge, The Hawaii Writers' Quarterly* are available for $16 per subscription series (4 issues).
Direct mail orders and catalogue requests may be addressed to:
Bamboo Ridge Press
P. O. Box 61781
Honolulu, Hawaii 96839-1781
808-599-4823

Library of Congress Cataloging-in-Publication Data
Yamanaka, Lois-Ann, 1961-
     Saturday Night at the Pahala Theatre / Lois-Ann Yamanaka.
          p.   cm.
     ISBN 0-910043-31-0   (pbk.) : $8.00
     1. Hawaii–Poetry.   I. Title
PS3575.A434S27   1993
811'.54–dc20
                                                                93-9139
                                                                CIP

10 9 8 7 6 5 4 3   95 96 97 98 99

Grateful Acknowledgment is made to the following publications in which some of these poems first appeared in slightly different forms:

Bamboo Ridge: The Hawaii Writer's Quarterly:
"Boss of the Food," "Kid," "Lickens," "Name Me Is," "Parts," "Tita: The Bathroom," "Turtles."

Hawaii Review: "Chicken Pox," "Girlie and Asi Frenz4-Eva," "Girlie: Monday Afterschool."

Michigan Quarterly Review: "Kala Gave Me Anykine Advice Especially About Filipinos When I Moved to Pahala," "Yarn Wig."

Parnassus: Poetry in Review:
"Saturday Night at the Pahala Theatre."

Puerto del Sol: "Empty Heart."

ZYZZYVA: "Prince PoPo, Prince JiJi."

The Anatomy of Water: A Sampling of Contemporary American Prose Poetry: ed. Steve Wilson, "Lickens."

Dissident Song: A Contemporary Asian American Anthology: ed. Marilyn Chin and David Wong Louie, "Haupu Mountain."

The Female Body: ed. Laurence Goldstein, "Kala Gave Me Anykine Advice Especially About Filipinos When I Moved to Pahala."

AUTHOR'S NOTE

This is a work of fiction. The characters here who interact
in the form of poetic novellas are the products of the
author's imagination. Any reference to real locales is intended
to give the work a setting in a historical reality.
Names and incidents are used fictitiously.

For Don Leland Sumada
and Melvin E. Spencer III,
my brothers,
look them
all in the eye.

CONTENTS

T H R E E

F O U R

ONE

Kala Gave Me Anykine Advice Especially About Filipinos When I Moved to Pahala

No whistle in the dark
or you call the Filipino man
from the old folks home across your house
who peek at you already from behind
the marungay tree, the long beans
in front of his face;

he going cut across your backyard
from the papaya tree side
when you whistle the Filipino love call,
then take you when you leave your house
for buy jar mayonnaise for your madda
from the superette.

Then he going drag you to his house,
tie you to the vinyl chair,
the one he sit on outside all day,
and smile at you with his yellow teeth
and cut off your bi-lot with the cane knife.
He going fry um in Crisco for dinner.
That's what Kala told me.

No sleep with your feet to the door.
No sleep with your hair wet,
Kala said, or you going be like Darlene Ebanez
who run around her house na-ked
and nobody can stop her when she like that.
She take her two fingers

and put um up her bi-lot.
That's what you not supposed to do, Kala said,
the Bible said so that's why.

No clip your toenails at night.
And no wear tight jeans or
Felix going follow you home with his blue Valiant
when you go plantation camp side past
the big banyan tree, past the sugar mill,
past the pile of bagasse, down your dirt road.
Kala said he rape our classmate Abby already
and our classmate Nancy even if he get one
girlfriend senior in high school
and his father one cop.

Kala told me no use somebody's deodorant
or I going catch their b.o.
No make ugly faces or my nose going be pig
and my eyes Japanee.
And no tell nobody the words she tell me.
Nobody. Especially the word she told me today.
Okay. Okay. The word is *cremation.*

The graveyard man he sew all the holes
on your body shut with dental floss, Kala said;
your eyes, your nose, your mouth,
your belly button, your okole hole
and yeah, even your bi-lot so the gas
cannot escape when he shove you in the brick oven.

Watch out for the Filipino man, Kala said,
he eyeing my black dog, Melba,
he eyeing my baby goat
that my uncle caught for me up Mauna Kea,
the small green papayas on my tree.

KALA GAVE ME ANYKINE ADVICE ESPECIALLY ABOUT FILIPINOS WHEN I MOVED TO PAHALA

Kala: Sitting on Our Bikes by the Catholic Church

You get yours yet?
Your rags, dummy.
You dunno what rags is?
Stupid, eh? Where you from?
Your madda neva tell you?
You neva see *Time of Your Life* fourth grade?
Faaack. I bet you wen' close your eyes, ass why.
When you get yours, you cannot ride bike, you know.
'Cause going be so-wa, stupid.
Of course I get mines.
I seventh grade already.
What grade you?
Sixth?
You going ge-et yours,
you going ge-et yours,
and going be all bloooooo-dy.

My madda told me they call um rags
'cause before time neva have Moddess
so they use the rice bags
and after they bafe,
they wash the rags in hot water.
No believe then, dummy.
I going tell all the old man wait for you
'cause you neva have yours yet
and you almost ripe.
Hoooo, tita, you better lock your doors
and pray to the Lord above
that you *neva* get yours
'cause I going tell
the old man that dinner
is almost ready to be served.

17

Kala: Captain of the Volleyball Team

Then he tell me, *When you going kiss me?*
We by the portables next to the teachers' cottages.
I standing between his legs,
he sitting on the railing
like the high school couples sit recess time
outside the science room.

School time he over there
with all the varsity volleyball boys
and he call me
when I getting my math book from my locker.
Eh, eh—he neva call me by my name—
and I no look at him
'cause I no like everybody know
I going with him and you guys, you assholes,
telling me, Go. *Jimmy boy calling you.*
And all the volleyball boys start laughing
when I run away down the hallway.

All dark and quiet by the portables.
Jimmy boy hold my hand
and look at my fingers one by one.
The other hand start rubbing my ass part
and I trying for pull away
but he pull me closer to him.
When you going kiss me? he ask again.
C'mon, I like kiss you. What.
You no like kiss me or what?
When you grad, I tell him. *At your grad party.*
Fuck, he tell. I can smell his mouth,
his face so close to mines.

Then, somebody shine the flashlight at us.
Was Mr. Shimayama. I dunno where he came from
but I figga he was going home
to the teachers' cottages after the volleyball game.
Howzit, Jimmy boy, he tell.
Good game, brah. You had some good digs in the back.
I know he trying for see my face
but I stay hide um
bumbye he tell my uncle
and I catch lickens from him.
My uncle, he no scared lick me.
He just wail anything that close to his hand
when he get piss off like the other time
Mr. Shimayama tell him I futting around
with the boys in our math class.

So Jimmy grab my two ass cheeks
and make his eyebrows go up and down at Mr. Shimayama.
Then Shima laugh one funny kine laugh
and tell, *Be good, eh, Jimmy boy.*
I turn little bit and see the flashlight go up
and down on the sidewalk, across the hibiscus bushes
then it gone.
Okay then, Jimmy boy tell me.
I not going kiss you.
I going do something else.
Small kine. No so-wa. I promise.
Then he by my neck.
All hot his mouth over there.
Long time he sucking the same spot.
That's one hickey, he tell me,
so all the boys know you mines.
I scared 'cause he start getting any kine with me.
No. No, I tell him but he pull me more hard.
Leggo me, Jimmy boy. I going home.
And I run all the way home.

My uncle waiting 'cause the game wen' pau
kinda long time ago.
Where you was? he yell
when he see me by the front lawn.
Then he turn on the porch light.
You fuckin' little slut, he yell
and he slam the screen door.
He grab the hose pipe and start licking me
on my face and my back.
I know where you was,
you little bitch.
Get in my house.

He pull my hair to the kitchen sink
and grab one Brillo pad.
Then he drag me to the bathroom.
You see that thing on your neck?
You see um?
And I wen' look at um.
I promise. I neva know was that purple,
the thing Jimmy boy did to me.
Here, take this Brillo and scrub your neck
till all that gone.
That's dead blood, he tell.
And he start scrubbing um.

Oweee, oweee, I yelling.
Shut up. Shut up, he yell.
Then he make me do um.
Pretty soon, all raw my neck.
Not bloody, you know, stay white
with small red dots
and clear yellow liquid dripping
from one cut the size
of one silver dollar.
I tell you, my uncle say,

that punk you was with
get one like you
and I going Brillo his neck, too.

My uncle pick up his flat brush
and whack my head plenny times.
Uncle, uncle, I tell him.
I neva like.
I promise.
I neva know.

You one liar, he tell me,
one fuckin' little liar.
You loved it.
Every goddamn minute of it.

Kala: Saturday Night at the Pahala Theatre

I was shitting 'cause the theatre lady,
she own the store where us buy slush afterschool
and she know I only seventh grade
'cause her daughter our classmate, Nancy.
NNNAaannccy. The *one*—the one told us she had policeman
in the sixth grade. *Policeman*.
Fuzz, brah, fuzz. Yeah, you neva know?
The theatre lady is her *madda*.

She look at me *long* time
when she rip my ticket in half.
Then she give me one real long piece toilet paper
for wipe the soot from the sugar mill off my seat.
Last time you and me went,
she gave us small piece, rememba?
And when I went home, I wen' catch lickens
from my uncle 'cause my pants was all black.

Mugs walk first then Jimmy boy push my back part
for follow him. He walk close behind me.
All the old man sit in the last row.
I smell the tobacco they spit on the floor.
They laugh when I walk past
and say some words in Filipino.
I know they talking about me.
Jimmy boy push me again.

Of course neva have cartoons.
You stupid or what?
You neva seen one X-rated movie before?

Me too.   Okay.   No tell nobody, okay?
Had five cheerleaders 'cause the movie
was *Cheerleaders Growing Up.*
They all was haole
and they was on one picnic table
like the one we get at school.
They all was telling their stories.

Had one, her was call to the office
'cause she was one bad girl smoking cigrettes
in the bathroom.   The fat, bolohead principal,
he make her all scared. He say he going tell her fadda.
So the cheerleader, she all nuts, right?
He say he fix everything for her.
But he tell her
she no can tell nobody.

Then the teacher, he one man, he come in
the office.   He wearing a suit with one tie.
The principal, he sweating already so he wipe his glasses.
The teacher, he one real worm.
He tie the cheerleader to a chair.
He tell her, *Don't be scared,*
and he gag her mouth.

Then the principal, he take off her shirt
and she crying.   Her eyes all black underneath
from her eyeliner.   Then he take off her bra
and the teacher suck her.
For *real.* I *saw* um.

Don't cry, he say *or we're going to have to tell
your father what you did,* the principal say.

Jimmy boy hand go on my leg
and he look at me long time.
I no look at him.
I like do that to you, he tell.
Mugs, he laugh and make his eyebrows go up and down
at Jimmy boy. *Me and Mugs, maybe.*
Come my house with us in the back by the shed,
he say. *I going do that to you.*

I try get up for buy popcorn or use the bathroom
or something. But Jimmy boy grab my wrist
and hold me down to the seat.
You sit right here, he tell.
So you can learn.
I shut my eyes.
Had four more cheerleaders.

Kala: Grad Party

Uncle drag my arm to the garage.
Get coconut leafs with anthurium
and red ginger all around the sides.
Jimmy boy father fishing net
and plastic floaters hanging there too.
Some Hawaiian guys playing music so loud
everybody gotta scream when they talk.

Uncle make me sit next to him
on the picnic table cover with luau paper.
From way the other side, I see Jimmy boy.
He get plenny lei on.
Fuck, my uncle tell. *Why you neva make lei
for Jimmy boy? Had plenny puakenikeni in the yard.
Here. Fast kine. Sign my name on this card.
Hurry up, shit. Jimmy boy coming over here.*

Eh, Jimmy boy, uncle yell.
Con-gra-choo-lations.
They shake man-style
and hug fake kine like men do.
*Go get me and Jimmy boy one beer.
We going get real drunk tonight, right, Jimmy boy?
Get the beer then beat it,* uncle tell.
*Only the men stay outside and drink.
Here, Jimmy boy, toast. To your fuu-cha.
Beat it,* uncle tell. *When I pau drink,
I come get you.*

I stay with all the small kids in the house.
We watching tv.
Jimmy boy come by the picture window.
He stare at me.
He give me one head jerk like *Come here.*
Your uncle like you, Jimmy boy tell. *Right now.*

I go out the back door.
My uncle he all drunk awready.
He talking with Mr. Freitas the ag teacher.
Ho, Jimmy boy, uncle slur. *Come here.*
Where your Bud?   Toast with us.
They all three guzzle um down.

Then Jimmy boy tell, *Eh, I going take*
your niece down you guys' house
get her yearbook, okay?
I stay shake my head behind Jimmy boy, *No, no.*
My uncle, he ignore me.
Sure, sure, Jimmy boy, he tell.
Eh, he yell at me,
Jimmy boy going take you down the house.
Move it before he make you walk.

Here, here, Jimmy boy, uncle tell with sweet voice,
one mo toast. To your fuu-cha.
May it be bright and full of sunshine
from the dear Lord above.
Uncle real drunk. *Amen,* he tell
and all the men laugh.

Jimmy boy take me in the blue Dodge Dart.
He take me Punalu'u by the ponds.
Dark over there.
The air smell salty.
What you going give me for my graduation? he tell.
He sit so close to me,
my face stay press to the window.

You neva give me nothing yet.
I no say nothing.
If you no give me nothing,

I going take something from you
and what I take,
you neva going give nobody else
ever again.

Like what? I tell.
I no mo nothing you like.
Oh yeah? he tell
and his big hand
reach under my dress.
I close my eyes tight
and turn my head.
It hit the window hard.
Relax, he tell.
This not going hurt at all.

Tita: The Bathroom

Try pass me my bag.
Shit, real rabbit fur.
I bought um at Project 3, the hippy store.
Had all kine calas too. I wen' pick this black one
so no get dirty when I use um.
You seen Jojo's bag? The white one?
All brown the fur.
Mo worse, she get the nerve still use um.
I wen' tell her, *So what, Jojo—*
you wen' use your bag for wipe your ass?
Looks fuckin' brown to me.
Nah, she neva say shit.
Think she going answer back to me?
I broke her face then make her eat
that brown rabbit bag for lunch.
I should have told her that, yeah?
What Jojo, you like eat rabbit?

Eh, light the incense before I light my cigrette.
I like the coconut incense the best.
I wen' try um all—the blueberry, the strawberry.
The hippy man in the store wen' ask me,
Are you planning to smoke some marijuana, man?
I tole him, *What you tink, fucka—*
I buy these for fun?

Like drag? You the stalest ass I eva met.
If you not going smoke,
then why you follow me in the bathroom for?
You so stupid. I bet you dunno even what one joint look like.
Hea. This the rolling paper and this the buds—
you just plain stupid, yeah?
You eva wen' smoke dope or what?
You stale. Ass all I can say about you.

'Kay, you hold um between the pointa finga
and the thumb, not like one cigrette
or can tell you out of it.
Take notes, you stupid shit.
Breathe in deep drag like this. Hold um in.
Eh, gotta talk with stuck ass voice
otherwise everybody going know you dunno how for smoke.
Shaddap already. Then you let the smoke out slowly.
I going save the rest of this joint
for the county fair next weekend.

You saw Chris looking at my tits in English?
He so horny. When he was giving his report,
I seen him checking me out.
What you laughing at, asshole?
Tink it's funny, eh?
Why—you just jealous 'cause your tits
look like mosquito bites.
You get the fuckinest flattest chest I eva seen.
Jap tits, invisible and small
like my bradda's. What your cup size?
Triple A? I betchu the butterfly
in between your cups mo big than your nipples.

Eh, I no wear low cuts on purpose.
Like me lick you right hea, hah bitch?
No get wise with me.
My shirts just stretch down
'cause I get the biggest motherfuckin' tits
in this whole school. You jealous
'cause I one Jap with melons
and you one Jap with plywood board.
But I no blame you 'cause if I had flat chest,

flat face, big ass and bubble eyes like you,
I would be jealous too.
Eh—you are fuckin' UGA-LEE.

Eh, where you go last period?
Carry my math book for me. Tanks, eh.
Bring um to the pickup ramp afta school.
If raining, you better not get um wet.
Ass one new Edgar Winter book cover.
I got um from Project 3, free of course,
'cause I buy plenny stuffs.
You think he one albino? Shit, go class.
I no mo time for explain to you what one albino is.
You the dumbest ass I eva met.
Nah, I the dumbest ass for hanging around with you.
Who gives a shit.
Go class.

Tita: Japs

I like see your strawberry musk.
Ho, I wen' put too much.
So what if the teacher look at us.
Just another stupid Jap. You eva wen' notice
that every teacher we had since elementry days
was one lady Jap?
Eh, what you trying for say to me?
I ain't one fuckin' Jap like them.
Their eyes mo slant than mine and yeah,
I one Jap, but not that kine,

the kine all good and smart and perfect
with their Japan pencil case,
leather saddle bag, smart math book,
muumuu every Friday
that the madda wen' sew, of course,
and the fadda drive one Torino.
That kine Jap is what I ain't.

But what you think about David?
Cute for one haole, eh?
But you know what I really think?
He like one local to me 'cause he surf.
I wen' ask him how he got his tan.
You blind or what? He get one *good* tan.
I hate talking to dummies like you.
You always acting stupid.
Now what I was saying?
Oh yeah, he told me he go surf down Honoli'i.
I wish he would ask me for *go* with him.
Gimme that strawberry musk.

Watch this. Watch me ask Lori for gum.
I like gum.   Eh, you so tight.
No need give me then.
She got doublemint up her ass at that store.
They get one store, you know.
Shit man, just 'cause she came from the mainland,
she think she can rule this class?
Her gramma had cancer, you know.
Ass why they gotta move Honolulu.
She get one skinny ass, yeah?

I wonder if her madda them can order
strawberry musk and makeup at the store?
Must be, 'cause Lori get all
the Maybelline Blooming Colors.
Fuckin' Jap slut. They the worse
'cause they like for act like they no poke.
But they do, 'cause can tell
by the way they walk funny.   Try watch.
Eh, Lori. Go shahpen my pencil.   Please.

Remember I told you Lance wen' try throw me
in the pool at that stupid party?
I only went 'cause David went.
You was there, eh? Well, you seen this then?
Why you always gotta act dumb?
Eh, what's your trip?
Just like you *like* hear me talk.

I wen' tell Lance, *Try throw me in the pool, fucka.*
My damn glue going come off.
Then I'm gonna have to break your face.
He's such a dick. Think he so hot shit.
Puny ass little Jap.

You know how long take me for put glue on my eyelid.
Plus my eye shadow and mascara.
Mo worse that night, I only had little bit glue
left in the tube, 'cause I went Longs
and neva have the white Duo glue.
Only had the black.
Ugly you know the black.

So anyways, I had for run to the bathroom all wet.
I wen' dig for one toothpick for put the glue.
Then I wen' pound that sink
'cause had only little bit glue left.
So I stay all rush and I line the glue
on my eyelid and paste the skin up,
but eh, my fuckin' face was all wet
so the glue came all bumpy.
I had for do um *all over again.*
Took one hour for look normal again.
I wish I had double eye.

I tell you, my next birtday,
when my madda ask me what I like,
I going tell her I like go Honolulu
for get one double eye operation.
I no care if all bruise
like Donna's one for six months.
Look Donna now, all nice her eyes,
and she no need buy Duo glue
or Scotch tape anymore
for make double eye.
I take the operation any day.

You heard what I told Emi?
I wen' tell her, *You fuckin' cow.*
I heard you was talking stink about me.
You like me kick your ass? C'mon, right now,

you stink little Japanee slut.
Nah. She wen' back off.
But I already went Penneys
for write her name on the chair.
For a good time, call Emi.
959-3311, the pride of Hilo town.

There. The bell wen' ring.
Spahk you tomorrow.
Bring your black nail polish. I like borrow.
The teacher wen' ask me yesterday,
Why do you paint your fingernails black?
I told her, *'Cause I like. Why?*
Fuck.   Fuck um all.
I no give a shit.

Tita: User

for n.b.

Eh—what you been saying about me?
That I use your stuffs and no return um?
Eh—no act. I no mo your Donny Osmond 8-track.
I hate *Down by the Lazy Riva.*
And I no mo your Captain and Tenille tape either,
so get off it. I so piss off right now
I like buss all the tapes
I *did* borrow from you.

No get *wise.* No ac-cuse.
'Cause when you ac-cuse,
you *act* like I *use,*
and I no use, I borrow.
Stupid, I get your Tower of Power,
Wild Cherry and Full Moon tapes
and I get your *Traces of Love long ago,*
Spill the Wine dig that girl,
and your *Playground in My Mind*
my name is Mi-kol
I got one ni-kol forty-fives
and that's all, asshole.
So no blame.

And no. I dunno who the fuck
took your madda's Lettermens and Percy Faith tapes.
And the Ray Conniffs, that I *did* take
'cause I wanted for hear *Precious and Few*
but I wen' return um last Monday
when I seen you in home ec
and you wen' put um in your backpack,
the one with the mushrooms on top.
So no act. And tell your madda no act too.

See the problem with you and her
is that you guys blaming me
like I wen' use all your 8-tracks
when the fack-of-the-matter is
you guys tapes was all stretch out and wa'p-ted
before I wen' even touch um.

And I wen' let Nish
use your *Partridge Family Christmas* album
so she get um. Go blame her.
And was my bradda wen' broke
the *Point Me in the Direction of Al-ba-ker-kee* record
'cause he thought was mine,
and he was piss off at me,
but wa'p-his-jaws was yours.

Yeah, go 'head. Blame me some mo.
Pretty soon I going have to get all bo-bo
and buss your mouth for blaming.
I *no mo* your Archies comics.
And anyways, you said I could take
any Archies I like, plus any Richie Rich
or Casper the Friendly Ghost.
You so tight, I no can believe.
And you one fuckin' Indian giver.

And all those Kahlil Gi-bran cards you shown me,
no ac-cuse like after I wen' touch um
you neva seen um again.
And so what if you seen Eugene Fong with the one
Love-Me-for-What-I-Am-Not-for-What-You-Want-Me-to-Be card.
You no think I can go down Book Gallery
and get my own cards?
How you so damn sure ass yours,
ass what I like know.

And the La-nard Nimoy one
If-You-Are-My-Friend, Trust-Me, Love-Me-Inside-and-Out,
eh, take those words to heart, *friend,*
'cause I dedicate this card to you
for let you know from my heart
how you hurt me, you asshole,
when you no can even trust me
with some of your stuffs.

And *no*, I neva take your blue bikini panty,
the one says *Friday* on top with black roses,
and I piss off to the max about this one,
'cause look your skinny ass
and look my fuckin' fat ass
and tell me straight—
how the *hell* could I get my ass
in that blue bikini panty
without getting the worse Portagee torture
I eva had in my *whole* life?
Ass what I like know.
And no tell me the bugga stretch
plenny 'cause I tell you what—
somebody else's *used panty*
is the last place
I would *eva* like put *my* cho-cho.

Tita: On Fat

Eh, what you trying for say?
That I one fat cow? Well, fuck you.
I ain't fat. I just more mature than you guys.
You guys ain't developed yet.
I bet you neva even get your rags yet.
All you guys a bunch of small shit Japs.
Anyways, look at you, asshole.
Think you so slim? You fuckin' fat too,
especially in the ass.
Besides, no get wise with me
for I tell Craig what Leland told you.
Think I wen' forget, eh?

Rememba, Leland told you Craig get one small dick
'cause he seen um in Mr. Yanagi's P.E. class?
Look like one Vienna sausage
and you guys giving him the thumbs up sign
like *Howzit-Craig-what's-up*
when actually you guys teasing his dick size.
So go 'head. Wise up with me, asshole.
I tell him today, right now you like.
Okay then. No get wise.

You—you just like Nancy.
You guys think you so skinny
when you guys is so fuckin' fat.
Shit, I like punch you guys' face
when I see you acting slim.
You wasn't shame take off your shirt
when us went down Leileiwi for swim or what?
Eh, your bikini was so down-the-road.
What you wanted for do?

Act in front of the tourist boys that was there?
You and your damn fat friend, Nancy,
you guys look so stupid
'cause you was the only one
in the whole gang who wen' take off their shirt
when all us wen' leave ours on
for jump in the water.
You neva see the tourist boys laughing at you?

Where you got those stupid *greeen* hiphuggas from?
Wigwam? Kress Store? Cheap sale, eh?
Shit, pull um up.
Can see your ass crack.
You so damn fat and you trying for wear those pants.
Give it up, girl.
You ain't made for clothes like that, fat ass.
Mo worse, you get the nerve for wear halter top.
What—you made that in your Singer sewing class
or your gramma made um with leftover blanket material?
Eh, you look so stupid.
And mo worse, you think you look slick.

We go eat lunch. I so damn hungry.
I stay staavving to death.
I only been eating chicken noodle soup
for dinner. 'Cause I on one diet, stupid.
You for ask dumb questions.
I getting piss off at you.

Yeah and I piss off at my madda too.
Stink ass witch, I told her I was on one diet
and I wen' ask her for buy me some Campbell soup
but her she neva buy me shit.
So I had for drink the juice from my bradda's saimin.
I wanted to shove the noodles
down my throat but no can, eh?

Mo worse, my madda stay telling me,
Eat carrots or celery. Shit,
I wanted to tell her for shove that carrots
up her tight ass.

I dunno, I too fuckin' fat.
Eh, no say I not fat,
when I *know* you think I fat,
'cause that only makes me *mo*
fuckin' mad.

Tita: Boyfriends

Boys no call you yet?
Good for you.
Shit, everybody had at least
two boyfriends already.
You neva have even *one* yet?
You act dumb, ass why.
All the boys said you just one little kid.
Eh, no need get piss off.

Richard wen' call me around 9:05 last night.
Nah, I talk *real* nice to him.
Tink I talk to him the way I talk to you?
You cannot let boys know your true self.
Here, this how I talk.
Hello, Richard. How are you?
Oh, I'm just fine. How's school?
My classes are just greeaat.
Oh, really. Uh-huh, uh-huh.
Oh, you're so funny.
Yes, me too, I love C and K.
Kalapana? Uh-huh, uh-huh.

He coming down from Kona next week.
He like me meet him up the shopping center.
Why, you like see him?
He one fox with ehu hair.
I know he get ehu hair
'cause he wen' send me his picture.
What you said?
Of course he know what I look like.
Eh, what you trying for say?
That I one fuckin' fat cow?
Yeah, he get one picture of me.

41

I wen' send him the one of us by the gym.
The one us made you take for the gang
'cause us neva like you in the picture.
Nah—I was in the back row
so I wen' look skinny, eh.
Only had my face.

I get this guy wrap around my finger
'cause of the way I talk on the phone.
I told him I get hazel eyes and I hapa—
eh, I pass for hapa ever since I wen' Sun-In my hair.
Lemon juice and peroxide too.
Ass why all orange and gold.
Plus when I glue my eyes and make um double,
my eyes ain't slant no mo
and I swear, everybody ask me,
Eh, you hapa?

So what if not all true?
How he going know from that picture I gave him?
I was so far in the back.
He said he get um in his wallet.
And no be acting all cute when he come.
Just shut your mouth
and let me and him do whatevas.
I warning you now, no get stupid.
And no follow us if he like go cruising
'cause something might happen
in the car. I get um.

I get um good.
'Cause I know what boys like do
and it ain't hanging around the gym
or swimming laps after school

or sitting around the shopping center eating slush
with fuckin' losers like you,
I tell you that much.

So you keep writing Elmer's name
inside your folders and prank calling him,
and dedicating songs to him
and writing him stupid letters signed ano-namous
and shoving um in his locker.
Eh, think I stupid?
Everybody know you like Elmer.
And everybody know you the dumb ass
doing all those dumb things.
How they know? 'Cause maybe I told um.
Why. You going make something of it?
I would *love* to have to kick your ass right now.

Yeah, I told um. I told um all.
And you like know what?
You better give up all that shit
and grow up 'cause everybody,
all the boys think you just one small kid
and no boy going eva be your boyfriend
'cause you dunno how
for make your voice all nice,
your face all make-up,
your hair all smooth and ehu,
your clothes all low cut,
and your fingernails all long.
You dunno how for act.
And you, you just dunno how for please.

TITA: BOYFRIENDS

Girlie: Monday Afterschool

You know what?
Boy wen' beef with Keoni
by the county pool
and you know what he did?
He wen' say, *C'mon Keoni, you fucka, right hea.*
Then Boy wen' take off his shirt
and fly um on the fence.
Then he wen' take off his pants!
I no joke you. Then he wen' beef
Keoni bare balls.

After that, I wen' tell Boy,
Eh, cool head, boo. Why you wen' take off
your pants? Everybody was laughing—
all the cheerleaders
and jv players, boo.

And Boy wen' tell me all mad,
'Cause that's how my fadda fight
my uncle them when they all drunk.
They no like their clothes come rip
so they fight bare balls,
I no joke you—no bee-ba-dees 'n all,
my fadda them.

Then after that, I wen' treat Boy
hot dog and large slush at Country Mart
'cause he neva have no money.
And all the way home,
I no could stop thinking about
how Boy could've beef
all na-ked. *Suckin' guy,*
I wen' tell him, *all the girls*
seen your grapes.

Girlie and Faso Face the Music

After school on Wednesdays,
Faso and me ride our banana bikes
past the old Pahala Hospital,
past the Methodist Church,
for go hula lessons.
Sometimes, the Japanee man,
his billy goat loose and he chase us,
with his big horns low to the ground.
Faso and me pedal all our might
with only one leg, the other one
on the handlebar so the goat no butt us.
And Faso, she screaming, telling the goat,
Yeah, you sucka, hit me, hit me.
And she laugh all the way

to Aunty Alice hula studio,
where we hear Aunty's phonograph
play "Sassy" for the small girls.
Us wait for our class to start.
Faso tell me jump and pull the branch
on the shower tree to the ground
so I can slingshot her to the sky.
But Faso, she too fat, I think in my head.
She going broke the branch
and pau for all us,

no can play.
But I scared tell Faso no.
Bumbye next time we go swimming pool
and Sonny, the lifeguard, not looking,
she pull down my bikini bottom
and yell at her cousin,

Alberto, Alberto, Berr-tooo.
Look.   Quick.   Look her white ass.
And Faso pull my swim cap so the rubber flowers
all come off and she yelling,
Alberto, Berr-tooo. Look the water lilies.

So I jump high for the V branch
and put um all the way to the ground.
Pull um back, Faso tell me,
mo back, mo back, quick before
Aunty Alice see us and us gotta dance
by ourself in front the whole class.

So I pull um hard.
You ready, Faso, I tell her.
Okay—one—two—tree.
But the bugga when snap back,
Faso and all, branch and all, on me.
Aunty Alice stay screaming all kine words in Hawaiian
and yelling, *You wait, cun-funnit,*
I going tell your fadda, you fat Portagee, you.
And you, you damn Japanee, she yelling at me,
I see you hiding behind that tree.
Get in here and face the music. Now. *Both of you.*

Faso stay rubbing the scratches
on her ass part and her legs.
And when I wen' look good,
Faso's pants was rip and her panty too.
Mo worse, her ass was kinda bleeding
and Aunty stay yell some mo,
Good for you, good for you, I hope so-wa.

Then what Faso said,
I no could believe, and brah, I was right there.
She wen' yell *back* at Aunty,

GIRLIE AND FASO FACE THE MUSIC

Aw fuck you, you fuckin' ka-naka.   Bite my fut.
Shit, I tell my fadda come shove this branch
up your ass, Aunty.   No yell at me.
And all the small girls stay stand behind
Aunty Alice and when Faso tell, *Eat this,*
and give Aunty the middle finger,
all the small girls gasp in
and some say, *A-ha-na-ko-ko-le-le.*

Faso look at me one long and hard one.
I see her bite the inside of her mouth.
Faso neva let one drop fall down from her eye.
You going hula lesson, or what? she ask me.

I wen' run away with Faso from hula lessons
that Wednesday and went the soda fountain
with her for drink vanilla Coke
and half one hamburger deluxe.
Good we no need go hula lesson, I tell her.
Faso no talk. *I hate Aunty,* I tell some mo,
and I hate the old hula building.
Faso still no talk. She just eat slow kine.

Ay, but us cannot go uniki now
and ay, us probly not going the Hilo and Maui trip.
I no look at Faso.
I bite my fingernail off.
That's when Faso wen' give herself
her own nickname
which was Faso,
short for Fat-Asso, she said,
and I neva even laugh.

GIRLIE AND FASO FACE THE MUSIC

Girlie and Asi Frenz4-Eva

I tell you something.
No tell nobody, okay?
You know the pervert by the school
who wear the big rain jacket and jag off
in front the small girls
when they walk to school?
The one—he everytime by the trash bin.
Anyway, one time, me and Asi was walking up there
and the guy start yelling Asi's name.
So I wen' tell her, *Eh, the fuckin' haole pervert*
stay calling you.

What? You like again?
she wen' yell back at the guy.
The guy start rubbing his tits and pointing at Asi.
Well, hurry up. I ain't got all day, she wen' tell.
Then the guy start running to us.
I stay pull Asi's arm but she no move.
I stay tell her, *What you doing, Asi?*
The fucka is running to us. Let's go.
Ho, I dunno, next thing I knew, he was right by us.
All stink he was like b.o.
and toe jam and halitosis
and oily hair all mix togeda, I no joke you.

C'mon, he stay tell Asi and he stay grabbing
for his dick part already. *Here's the 20.*
And he wen' take um out his pocket.
Then he wen' put um in between his teeth—
all ke-ke, his teeth, all yellow and full of plaque.
His hand stay grab his dick already.
I no joke you. Then you know what that fuckin' Asi wen' do?

I no could believe and brah,
I was standing right there.

She wen' unbutton her shirt, slow kine,
and the guy stay tell, *C'mon, c'mon,*
and then she wen' take off her bra,
slow kine, and the guy stay all nuts already,
his eyes stay rolling back.
And that Asi,
she wen' show the haole pervert her tits.
I no joke you, brah.
I was right there.
Ho, by that time, the guy was whackin',
like slappin' meat to the max.

And Asi wen' grab the money from the ground
'cause he wen' kind of bend over and groan.
She neva even button her clothes,
she stay hold um closed in the front,
telling me, *Run, Girlie, run! Hurry up!*
So we wen' run to the meat market
and Asi wen' buy tree packs Kools
and one large pack Doublemint, two bottle Pepsi,
and one big party size Funyuns for me and her.

I wen' grab one handful of Funyuns
and put um all on my fingers
like we always do, but wen' taste funny.
Wen' taste like onion breath, I no joke you,
like stink mouth and halitosis in the morning.

Asi went home so I told her, *Laytahs.*
Me, I went to the school by the big tree.
Get the park benches over there, eh?
And I wen' look for the place I wen' carve
Girlie and Asi Frenz4-Eva.
Then I wen' scratch out the 4-Eva part
with my fingernails until no could see no mo.

TWO

Tongues

i.

You don't know what I feel inside.
Sit in this dark closet
with dry cleaner plastic hanging,
and old straw bags
with shiny white shells on top,

old eyelet dresses, an orange one
with a satin sash only Mama
know how to tie right,
sitting here, waiting here,
'cause my sista told me to,

and there's her nose and her mouth
in the crack of the closet door,
her tongue pointing the way
only she can make her tongue point
and whispering my name, *lllll,*
put your tongue all fat and round,

put your tongue to mine.
She say to me:
    We going shine,

    you and me, shine
    in the darkest places
    SHINE.

It's all wet in here,
humid and heavy, the clothes smell
like four times worn without washing,
like sista's purple blanket
hiding under her dirty pillow;
I put my fat tongue out,

right by the crack
in the closet door,
touch it to her pointy tongue
like she says and close my eyes.

ii.

We looking over the edge
of the cardboard box under
the garage sale table
in daddy's shop.

My sista is singing
strawberry fields forever
but she don't know
all the words.
She whistle the parts
she gotta skip, long
and breathy, I see
the sawdust moving in sunlight.

My KittyCat keep getting
pregnat, have four new babies
in the cardboard box.
They sucking KittyCat.

I pull the burlap bag
off of daddy's table and all
the screwdrivers, wrenches
and knifes fall off the side.

She say to me:
    I like this white one,
    the only white one KittyCat
    ever had. (she not singing this time)

Then she turns it over.
It's a boy, she says,
you can tell
get two tiny nuts there,

right there. I name him
Willy. Willy Mays.
She whistling again,
strawberry fields, the part

    let me take you down.

She start to pry the eye open.
Willy only three days old.
Right in the lean of sunlight,
into Willy gray eye.

I see it turning blue
right in front of my eye.
The cat squirm and screech.
KittyCat jump out the box.

Maybe he blind now.

    willy-one-eye blue and gray

See it? See it shine?
Maybe willy-one-eye blue and gray
see ghosts with his new eye.
See KittyCat licking it dry.

iii.

Today us tie each other to the clothesline.
You don't know what it feel like

when somebody like maybe your sista
pull the dishcloth tight around your mouth
while she telling you:

>   *watch me.*
>   *watch me.*
>   *very close now.*
>   *watch.*

She run get the short stepladder
from under the house and put it
in the tall ironweed by the clothesline.
Then I watch her run to daddy's shop
and get the rabbit cage
he made to take his bunnies

to sell to the old men across the street
and she run back to the clothesline.
She grab the bamboo fishing pole
next to the washing machine
and shove the fat end
into the top part
of the clothesline iron bar.

Some dust and dry leafs fall out,
then I hear something bigger shove slow
and babies crying being shoved out
of the clothesline.
Out come sparrow babies still in the nest
and she put um in the rabbit cage

right between my legs.
The mother sparrow come screaming
and dive bombing down and again,
pecking the cage and my leg

and the cage and my head.
I cannot cover my face;
I see my sista run by the washing machine;

she laughing so hard,
she grabbing grass outta the ground
and throwing it in the air,
football touchdown style.
When I look up,
I see the mother sparrow,
her pointy tongue moving up
and down in her screaming mouth,
her heading straight for my eye.

iv.

In the backseat of the Plymouth Duster
she say to me,

> *You get one old face and one old heart.*

I want to shove the paint rag,
      silver wet and all, up her tight ass
as she pick the canned cherries
off of day old pastries in Saran Wrap
on a styrofoam meat tray.
High-er. I light her knees with a butane lighter
      but she don't feel it
so I let it burn   and   burn   and   burn
and she feels it.

When she sees the flame, blue and orange tipped
      with black knee smoke, she slaps it
from my hands, so I call out our dead dog's name
the way I used to call her to come eat

with KittyCat some Purinas and Friskies
        mix together in the red dog dish,
side of Carnation milk and water;
I make my voice quiver
when I call our dead dog.

I make tears fall down until she turn
        her face to the Duster window, slump her head
til it hit the glass hard,
and she hold her stomach tight,
keep hitting her head

on the glass.
And I say:

        Shine, sista, shine.

v.

I in the old army blankets way,
way in the dark corner of daddy's shop.
I wiping the oil off of his tools
with the bottom of my shirt,

        sunlight seep through a hole in the wall, drill size.

My sista trying to find me,
        I hear her shuffling in the dry ti-leafs outside
        so I put my hands to my mouth
        all oily but I no care.
        I better not laugh too loud.

        *the world bend through a peephole like looking
        into the center of a marble.*

I hear her tantalizing me:

I going across the street to Edward house.
His mother going give me choclick ship cookies.
I going upstairs to Edward bedroom.

I thinking,

maybe I want to see my sista play
with Edward mind. He so rich
'cause his father work the plantation.
And Edward ride the company big,
white Ford truck with red tool box
in the bed and Edward wear
the father foreman hard hat.

So I say to her, *Come get me.*
I hear her but I cannot see her.
I hear her feet.

She coming up behind me.
She coming.
She grab me
by my hair
and bite my neck.

vi.

Here is our plan:

Paint our toenails and fingernails *shocking red*
and sit on the Twister game plastic sheet
on our driveway.

Sometime that all it take
to get Edward across the street.
My sista paint Edward toes.
I gotta hold the bottle Lemon Cutex remover

---

and a coupla cotton balls right by Edward,
otherwise he don't play this game.
Edward says when his father see
any red Cutex on him,
he force to do hundred pushups.

Plan Two:

    Sit on the same Twister game plastic sheet.
    Put two li hi mui seeds in the center
    of our lemon, and a third lemon
    with the package seeds
    on the side for Edward see.
    This going get him for sure.

Here he come.

vii.

I not so sure
what to do.
I follow my sista.
She point
her pointy tongue at me.

Edward ask
if he can have
the third lemon plus
two seeds.
She sucking and sucking
and licking and slurping her lemon.
She motion with her eyes for me do the same.

I put my round tongue tip
in the center of my lemon, roll
my eyes back and purr.
Edward watching with his mouth

open, his fat tongue moving
slowly across his lip,
gotta suck in the spit,
he want this so bad.

She say:
> For the first seed, Edward,
> you gotta eat one Friskies nugget
> from KittyCat red dish.

Go get um, she tell me.
Get black ants all over um and crumbly.
I run back and give um to my sista.

She hold the li hi mui in one hand
and the Friskies in the other.

> This Friskies for this li hi mui.

Edward hold his breath and crunch the Friskies.
Sound delicious like soda crackers,
like choclick ship cookies.

> No no no. Not yet.
> (Edward whining for his seed)
> You gotta eat two more Friskies
> for the second seed.

She hold the seed high in the sunlight.

> Go, she command me. Go get two
> Friskies nugget for Edward.

All crumbly and ants all over the Friskies
and Purina Cat Chow in the red dish.
Edward crunch,

crunch,
    crunch,
    crunch,
    crunch
five times for the two nuggets
get small enough for go down.

> *And then. Now Edward.*
> *No   no   no.*
> *You cannot have the two seeds yet.*
> (Edward almost ready for run home
> to his upstairs room
> with toybox with his name on top.)

So I say,

> *Almost, Edward.* Lucky he believe me.

My sista say,

> *Come.   Come, Edward.*
> *No   no   no.*
> *You gotta follow me*
> *on your hands and knees*
> *like a dog or maybe a cat, whatever animal*
> *you want to be.*

Edward crawling across the driveway.

viii.

We in the dark corner of daddy's shop.
We sitting on the Twister plastic.

> *Put your right foot in (the red dot.)*
> *Put your left foot in (the green dot.)*

Put your right hand in (the yellow dot.)
Put your left hand in (the bluuuue dot.)
That's what it all about.

Edward is twisted.

You cannot move or else
No lemon. (sucka, sucka)
No li hi mui. (coupla slurps)
No li hi mui. (she lick her lips
  with her pointy tongue)

I wiping the knife with the oil.
My sista gag Edward
with a Suck-Um-Up t-shirt.
Edward no move.
My sista tell me
cut the front of his t-shirt
right down the front.
His eye telling me
his daddy going crack him.
(Noooo. Please NO.)
I cut um open.

My sista flicking the metal snaps
on Edward pants.
(she whistling too what else)

  FLICK.
        FLICK.
               O-PEN.

She pry the zipper open
tooth by tooth;
we hear um together like
in slow

motion,
            slow motion.
And she yank it off his legs.

>   *Put your right hand*
>   *in the yellow dot!*
>   *Put your left hand back.*
>   *In the bluuue dot!*
>   *Put the knife* oil and all
>   *on his neck.*

Edward, he no move.
Off with the bee-ba-dees
and my sista make me put um over
Edward face. I press
the knife on his neck.

And for the first time
I seen um.
The nuts and the ding
up close. *Look,*
my sista say,

>   *All the veins and it's purple and pink*
>   *and get one edge at the top part,*
>   *like one helmet.*

We giggle.

I touch the nuts.
It roll like a big spider egg
trapped in skin.
And the ding growing and growing
right in my sista hand.
My tongue
come flicking outta
my mouth.

Parts

PAIN IN PARTS

THE BRAIN

I get one
splitting
headache.
No ask me questions.
And no move.
First one
who breathe
going get
one good whack
with the fly swatter.
You. Cook the rice.
You. Fry some Spam.
Open one can corn.
Everybody
shut up.
I work all day long,
I come home
and all you doing
is watching tv.
Sit down.
Shut up.
I gotta rest.

THE FACE

Stop muttering
under your breath
before I pound
your face.
Want me
to punch
your face in?
You cannot
run away
from me.
Try.
I catch you
and give you
double lickens.
Now get
your ass
in your room
and fold
all the laundry.
Then iron
your father's shirts.
Go. The laundry
is on your bed.
Hurry up.

THE EYE

I
found
this letter
in your
panty drawer.
Did you write
all these evil things?
Looks like your
handwriting.
Like me read this
to Judy and her mother?
Like me call them up
come over for lunch
right now?
What you mean,
no, wait?
So you did
write it.
I
cannot believe
that so much evil
can live
in one person.
You are a evil child.
You are filthy.
You are a hypocrite.
Stay in your room.
Forever.

ii. BLAME IN PARTS

THE NOSTRIL

What I told you
about digging your nose?
Who taught you that?
You going get
two slaps
I ever see you
doing that
in public again.
Good for you
your nose bleed
and I hope you get
so-wa stomach too
for eating that shit.
And your uncle,
next time I see him,
he going get
two slaps too
for teaching
you damn kids
to eat your hanabata.
Gunfunnit.

THE FOOT

Who the hell
wen' use
my rubber slippers?
Gotta be somebody
with toe jams.
You?   You?   You?
Then who, gunfunnit?
The damn ghost?
Gotta be one of you clowns
'cause I no mo toe jams
and I was like that
since I was small.
Here, smell this shoes.
No mo stink, eh?
Here.   You.
Wash this with Clorox
and hang um
on the clothesline
in the sun.
Maybe the smell go 'way.
And if I catch
the asshole
who using my
rubber slippers
and making me
catch their toe jams,
I going broke their ass.

THE MOUTH

Whoever ate
all the meat
from this stew
is asking for it.
Who the hell
took all the meat
and left
the vegetables and soup?
Gunfunnit.
I put three trays meat
and all gone.
Let me see your plate.
You.   Let me see.   YOU.
YOU the one.
You damn pig.
Why you neva
leave some meat
for the rest of us?
Next time, I going put
three trays meat
and chop up
your damn dog too
so get meat
for everybody.
You like me do that?
Then no get greedy.
You guys piss me off.

THE ASS

Who you slutting
around with?
You better not
be a whore
or you going find
your ass passed around
from one Joe
to the next.
She give, you know.
They all going know
how easy you are
and you going think
they love you
and you going think
you popular
but all they thinking
is you spread fast.
They going say,
I love you
I love you
c'mon let's do it.
And what you going say?
Girl, you better say no,
you going wait
until you married.

THE CRACK ONE

What are you
trying to do?
You no mo shame
always sitting
in dark corners
with Fely's brother?
Fely my friend, you know,
and you, you goddamn
12-year-old slut
sitting in dark corners
with that 19-year-old
brother of hers.
What he was trying for grab
from between your legs?
Think I wasn't looking, eh?
Gunfunnit.
No tell me
the deck cards.
Why you put
the deck of cards
between your legs
when you know
he wanted um?
You wanted him
for touch your crack?
Answer me.
Answer me.

THE CRACK TWO

Why you had to tell me this?
Don't look at me.
Yeah, you better hang your head.
Don't you ever talk
about this again.
Don't tell nobody.
Nobody.
You hear me?
Don't ever tell your father.
What you expected?
You little cock teaser.
This is what you get.
You deserve it.
He one 19-year-old man
and you bending over
right in front his face.
What the hell did you expect?
Where he took you?
Why-did-you-follow-him-there?
What did I say
about going into
a man's room?
You liked it?
Felt good?
Say it louder.
So-wa?
Good for you.
Now you a *ho-a*.
You not a virgin.
Nobody
going love you.
Nobody
going marry you.
Everybody

going use you.
Once you know
what it feels like,
you going want it
everytime.
You neva
going be able
to stop
yourself.
Dirty girl.
Dirty
girl.

iv. WHAT THE HANDS DO
ABOUT ALL OF THESE PARTS

ADVICE FROM A 14-YEAR-OLD FRIEND

Take the needle. Take it.
Cut your arm. Cut.
See. You feel no pain
'cause you already so-wa inside.
Keep going. Make plenny lines,
as much as you can take.
Feel good, yeah?
Feel icy, yeah,
when the needle break your skin?
Push um deep, the needle,
till you see the white part
of your meat. Spread um—
spread the cut you just made
before the blood get hard.
Look inside. Trippy, yeah,
the small blood drops?
How your head?
Feeling white?
Kind of gray, yeah the feeling?
Going away, the pain inside,
'cause you getting numb.
Your whole body not throbbing yet?
I remember the first time
I did this. Felt so good
when my whole body was going
and the blood started dripping
on my leg and my friend
wen' tell me taste um,
'cause that's me coming out
of myself. Tasted like rust.
And I wen' forget about all the shit

that was happening to me.
My father took me emergency that day.
That was the first time
I seen him cry.
No. No need towel.
Lie down. Let the blood
drip on the sidewalk.
Then we write her name
with the blood
and when dry,
she going know
you was here
and she going know
how much you love her.

THREE

Boss of the Food

Before time, everytime my sista like be the boss
of the food. We stay shopping in Mizuno Superette
and my madda pull the Oreos off the shelf
and my sista already saying, *Mommy,*
can be the boss of the Oreos?

The worse was when she was the boss
of the sunflower seeds.
She give me and my other sistas
one seed at a time.
We no could eat the meat.
Us had to put um in one pile on one Kleenex.
Then, when we wen' take all the meat
out of the shells and our lips stay all cho-cho,
she give us the seeds one at a time,
'cause my sista, she the boss
of the sunflower seeds.

One time she was the boss
of the Raisinets.
Us was riding in the back
of my granpa's Bronco down Kaunakakai wharf.
There she was, passing us one
Raisinet at a time.
My mouth was all watery
'cause I like eat um all one time, eh?
So I wen' tell her, *Gimme that bag.*
And I wen' grab um.
She said, *I'ng tell mommy.*
And I said, *Go you fuckin' bird killa; tell mommy.*

She wen' let go the bag.
And I wen' start eating
the Raisinets all one time.
But when I wen' look at her,
I felt kinda bad cause I wen' call her bird killa.
She was boss of the parakeet too, eh,
and she suppose to cover the cage every night.
But one time, she wen' forget.
When us wen' wake up, the bugga was on its back,
legs in the air all stiff.
The bugga was cold.
And I guess the thing that made me feel bad
was I neva think calling her bird killa
would make her feel so bad
that she let go the bag Raisinets.

But I neva give her back the bag.
I figga what the fuck.
I ain't going suffer
eating one Raisinet at a time.
Then beg her for one mo
and I mean *one mo*
fuckin' candy.

Chicken Pox

My sista, she the best.
She wen' catch chicken pox las' week.
First, she had um only on her underarm.
Everytime I went in the living room,
she stay suffering on the vinyl couch
with her hands behind her head
and her chicken pox underarms all showing.
My madda tell her she no can scratch
otherwise going get scar.

Itchy? I tell her,
then I scratch my underarm for real kine
'cause I know make um mo itchy
when somebody scratch themself, eh?
Then, the underarm chicken pox went away
but guess what? She wen' catch chicken pox
on the rest of her body.
I bust laugh everytime I go in the living room
'cause stay all over her body,
even on her scalp.
Itchy?? I tell her.

Then, my other sista wen' catch chicken pox.
First, was only in her mouth.
She no could talk and she no could eat.
So I make one big bowl
of her favorite ice cream, mint chocolate chip,
and eat um right in front her face
even if that's my worse ice cream.
Her, she only cry 'cause itchy
and she no could scratch inside her mouth.

Then when the mouth chicken pox
went away, she got um on the rest of her body.
She stay lying on the same vinyl couch
the other sista was on, all itchy and hot.
I walk pass her and scratch my ass
by her face, all out kine.
Go 'way, you fucka, she tell me.
I'ng tell mommy.
Go. Go tell mommy, I tell her.
I scratch mommy's ass, too.
She cry 'cause she hot and itchy
and she going get lickens if she scratch.

But guess what?
Yeah, I wen' catch chicken pox, too.
But guess where I got um?
I had um only in my cho-cho.
I not lying. For real.
Shit, I was lying on the vinyl couch
for one week with my legs spread
so the thing heal more fast.
My sistas come in the living room
and scratch their cho-cho
full on, nuts out kine and laugh.
Itchy? they tell me.
Then scratch.

Yarn Wig

My madda cut our hair so short.
Shit, us look like boys, I no joke you.
I mean mo worse than cha-wan cut.
At least cha-wan cut get liddle bit hair
on the side of your face.
Us look almost bolohead
and everybody tease us, *Eh boy,
what time?* or *Eh boy,
what color your panty?*

I figga my madda sick and tired
of combing our long hair every morning.
She make us all line up
and us sit one by one on her chair
by her makeup mirror. She pull
and yank our hair just for put um
in one ponytail, but I tell you
she pull um so tight,
our eyes come real slant
and our forehead skin real tight.
Ass why now we get boy hair.

One time we stay walking home from school
and Laverne Leialoha calling us *snipe*
cause us Japanee and we get rice eye
she say. Then her and her friend write
S-N-I-P on the road with white chalk
they wen' steal from school.
Us dunno if she teasing us
SNIPE for Japanee or
SNIP for our boy hair.

My madda she start for feel sorry
for us but what she going do?
She no can make our hair grow back
all long again. But she go down Ben Franklin
one day and come home with plenny black yarn,
the thick kine. She make us yarn wigs,
I no joke you, with short bangs
and long, long yarn hair in the back,
all the way to our okole.
Just like the high school cheerleaders or
like Cher on the *Sonny and Cher Show*.
My sistas and me make the yarn hair
come in front then we flip um back
like Cher do.

The other day my madda took us store
and all us wen' wear our yarn wigs in the car.
We stay letting the yarn blow out the window
'cause so long. But when we was ready for go out,
I wen' fast kine pull off my yarn wig.
Shame, eh? More better they tease me,
Eh, boy, than *Eh, yarn for hair.*
My sistas, they so stupid,
they wear their yarn wigs in the store.
The lady at the soda fountain
tell, *Oh-ma goodness! So cute!*
Harriet, try come, try come,
and the lady from the fabric side
come running over.
Oh-la cute yo daughtas!
I kinda stay thinking maybe
I should have wore my yarn wig, too.
The fabric lady tell my madda,
You made um?
Oh you so cle-va wit yo hands!
And they so adora-bull.

YARN WIG

One sista start bringing her hair
in the front and acting like Cher.
My other sista pull all her hair on one side
and start acting like she looking
for split ends and her too go fling
her hair back.

Me, I order my vanilla Coke
and look at myself in the soda fountain mirror.
I see my sistas drag my madda
buy yellow and orange yarn
for make like Bewitch and Lucy.
I no look at myself no mo.
I pull my bangs real hard with both hands
and start feeling real bolohead.

Lickens

I neva like when she hit me with the iron hanger
'cause was so-wa. Mo so-wa than the wooden one.
So when she told my sista, *Go get the hanger,*
I always hope she would get one wooden one.
In fact, I wen' hope she would get the hanger
that I wen' put crochet on top in Miss Takata's class
for madda's day 'cause was soft.
I wen' try for make all the iron hangers crochet
but I wen' run out of yarn.
I neva have money for buy some mo.

Sometimes my sista was piss off at me
so she go bring the iron one
but I figga better cover my ass and no worry
about what kind hanger she brought.
Then my madda would say, *Move your arm.*
Move your arm. But I couldn't think fast
which was mo so-wa—
lickens on the arm or lickens on the ass.
So my madda hit my arm
'cause I covering my ass.
Lickens on the arm is mo worse
than lickens on the ass.

My madda, she tell my sista, *Go get the iron hanger.*
Then I know my madda real mad.
When she tell my sista, *Go get the wooden hanger,*
then I know she ain't that mad.
My stupid sista, everytime my madda tell her
go get someting for lick me with, she run.
I guess she neva like get lickens too.

Ho boy, one time my small sista wen' say *fut*
which we no could say 'cause the word
us had for use was *poot*
and she got lickens with the green brush
which was mo so-wa than the fly swatter
but both was less so-wa than the iron hanger.

My small sista everytime get lickens
'cause she always act dumb in public.
My madda wen' catch her looking
under the dummy's dress
in Edith's Dress Shoppe, downtown Hilo side.
So my madda wen' grab her
and ask her, *Whatchu doing?*
and my sista said,
Mommy, this lady no mo panty, and guess what?
My sista got lickens when we went in the car
'cause you cannot make shame in public.

No tell nobody, but one time,
my small sista wen' show her ching-ching
to one boy and she wen' get lickens with the golf club.
I dunno who wen' tell my madda.
I figga was the sista
that always run go get the hanger.
Must have been so-wa,
the lickens with the golf club.
But I dunno 'cause I neva do nutting that bad yet.

Dead Dogs R I P

My sista stay in the back of the garage
digging a grave for her egg-stealing,
all heartworms, coughing,
and stink breath dog.

Wiki wen' bite my friend Claude
on his ass 'cause he said fuck
in our house. My sista told him
no say f-word around Wiki
but Claude start screaming *fuckfuckfuck*
in my sista's face for fun
and Wiki wen' rush his ass, for real.
But now Wiki dead.

My sista came in the house
and wen' cry over and over
and louder and louder,
Wiki, Wiki, why you wen' die?
My madda had to slap her face couple times
so she snap out of it.

Me, I went outside
for check out Wiki's grave.
Had plumerias on top the dirt
and red anthuriums from my fadda's patch
and some bagasse sprinkle
on top the grave.
She put one cross
made from guava branch and rope
and she plant one kumquat tree
my fadda wen' plant
in the big cafeteria bean can.

And on the wall of the garage,
my sista wen' write,
W I K I   R I P
with the kiawe charcoal
from the smokehouse.

My sista come stand by me
next to the grave.
Me, I try for look sad,
but really, I hate Wiki.
Everytime, just for make me mad,
my sista used to whisper secrets
to Wiki when she mad at me
and act like they talking stink.
She tell, *Wiki, you know what I mean, eh,*
them, they so psst, psst, psst,
and she make Wiki nod her head
like *I know, I know.*
Then she laugh loud
and carry Wiki to her bed
for put her under the blanket
by the pillow and feed her
mint chocolate chip ice cream
from the same spoon,
dog spit and all.
Ass why I hate her.

But now, I no say nothing,
I just bow my head
like maybe I praying for Wiki.
Pretty soon, my sista pick up the kiawe
and write on the wall:

S U K I Daughter of W I K I hit by car
M A N A Fall from truck inter-no bleed
B U F F Y Soo-e-side

C L I F T O N Poison by Feda-rico
P E P E Big red dick, gave um away
M I D I Stolen at Kai Store
L I B B Y Dead on steps
C H E W I E Daughter of L I B B Y kidnap by Purto Recans
C H I C O ? Dunno
H O P P Y ? Dunno
H O P P Y J R. ? Dunno
D B Smash

And she write again:

W I K I   R I P

She put her face in her hands,
all charcoal all over,
and her whole body shake,
soft kine.

Prince PoPo, Prince JiJi

Shit. I hate my sista.
She no do her chores. She no do nothing.
My fadda tell her when he no stay, once a week
she suppose to dust all the stuff pheasants
on the shelf and wipe down the stuff pig wax tongue
on the living room wall. *Do your chores,* I tell her,
but her, she tell, *Shut your fat ass mout'*
and mine your own business.

But what I hate *hate* the most,
mo than my stupid sista,
is for feed the chickens.
I no mind feed Prince JiJi
and his hens, 'cause they tame.
Them, they live in the A-shape chicken coop
but daytime, they go all over
eating and shitting here and there.
So I go get the hen eggs
and put the mash in their dish.
I change the water 'cause chickens,
they fuckin' stupid; they shit in their own water.
Pretty soon along come Prince JiJi
and all his wifes for grind the mash.

Then the part I hate.
Gotta feed Prince PoPo and all his hens.
I no can even get the eggs
'cause as soon as he see me coming, Prince PoPo,
he get all nuts. He rush the wire of the chicken cage.
Him, he live in the two-story chicken house.
Us had ducks before on the first floor but now no mo.
Only Prince PoPo on the second floor part
acting like he one hot shit.

Me, everytime I lift the lid of the feedbox
and put the mash inside, Prince PoPo,
he peck my hand. *So-wa,* you know, one chicken beak
peck your hand hard kine.
Everyday I stay catching one or two pecks
on the hand and blood come out too.
So I tell all mad,
You fuck-in' *Prince PoPo,*
I hate *your guts. You stink shit chick-en.*
My sista watching me from my bedroom window.
She bouncing on *my* bed and yelling,
I hope the mosquitos bite your fat ass.

My madda start feeling all bad
'cause I catching dirty lickens from Prince PoPo
so she make me corn beef hash patties
for dinner and she make my sista go get
the green onion for the hash.

My fadda, he come home from the countryside
that weekend, and I stay cover
with calamine lotion.
I know I going get kakios all over.
My hands get at least
four Band-aid each with Mercurochrome.

My fadda, he tell, *Nuff awready.*
No need feed that goddamn chicken.
Look you, you no shame
you no can handle tings for me while I gone?
I thought you said you know how for take care?
Me, I no say nothing.

Next thing I know,
my fadda going outside by himself.
Us, we eat our corn beef hash patties with rice

and watch Ed Sullivan.
My fadda call me outside.
What, Daddy? I eating, I tell.
Come. Come with me right now, he tell.
What for? I tell him and I turn on the porch light.
My fadda, he get Prince PoPo neck in his hand
and the bugga stay dangling.
I going Bernard's Taxidermy Shop, he tell.
What for, I tell him.
He tell me, *I going stuff this asshole.*

When we get in the car,
I ask my fadda, *How you wen' kill Prince PoPo?*
I wen' trick him, he tell.
I wen' call him nice kine for eat some mo mash.
Then when he came for eat um,
I wen' inject his head with grass poison.
No could have big mark
bumbye Bernard no can stuff um.

My fadda, he put the stuff Prince PoPo on our TV.
Me, I wish he inject my sista head
and put her on the TV.
She still one asshole.
And Prince JiJi, when I go outside get the eggs,
I tell him be nice to me and his wifes
bumbye he gotta sit on our TV
with Prince PoPo, collecting dust
and watching us eat dinner.

Haupu Mountain

My madda she very mad at me today
because I answer her back with a sassy mouth.
She punch um with her big ring
so she no need hear me talk no mo.
And she say, *Get the hell outta this house*
and don't eva come back. Beat it.
Pack up your stuff
or I going send um to Salvation Army
so somebody can appreciate
all the nice shit you get.
Get outta my fuckin' sight.
That's why I here so early today, Bernie,
'cause I couldn't think of where else to go.

And Bernie, he close his taxidermy shop
and say, *Business slow today anyways.*
He take my small bag and carry um for me.
How come you get oranges in this bag? he tell.
I tell him that when my madda say beat it
out of this house, I neva know if I need food
or clothes so I grab some food from the icebox
in case I gotta sleep outside someplace
and I get hungry.

Bernie tell his wife make some musubi
and Vienna sausage. He tell her
we going hike up Haupu mountain.
If she like go, he tell, she can.
I hear them talking soft kine.
Then she say, *No need take me, Bernard.*
I gotta go graveyard today put flowas.
You two guys go.

I put your bag in the back bedroom, okay?
And I cook a special spare ribs dinner for you.
You watch. You going come back
and feel better, okay?

Bernie and me, we no talk too much today.
My face was getting real so-wa
so he put a bag of ice in a towel
and tell me put um on my face as we walk
through the big cow pasture.
It surround with ohia log fence and barb wire.
The grass is green and tall
like amber wave of grain, 'cept green.
The grass grow out of the eye socket of a cow skull.
Get bones and skulls all over.
Some cows and horses, they follow us
and I getting kinda scared, but Bernie,
he shoo um away. *No sked,* he tell.

Here, he say, *we go sit under this tree.*
This one pandanus tree.
I look up through the leaves and see some blue sky.
Bernie dust the ground for me.
Look. See how small the camp look from here.
He take out one musubi wrap in wax paper
from his knapsack and give um to me.
Then he take out the Vienna sausage and orange.
His wife had slice up the orange
I had in my bag for us eat.
Bernie pour some ice tea
from one long thermos for him and me share.

There my house, he say. *There the shop.*
Over there the Catholic church.
Where your house?   There.   Way over there.
I put the musubi on the wax paper in my lap.

And I look down at our camp and my house. Real small.
So small, I cover everything with my hands
and no see nothing at all.

Pueo Don't Fly

Bernie let me touch the glass eyes
in the tray at his shop.
He order um from a magazine call *Van Dyke*.
He tell sheeps and goat get the same eye.
Chinese ring neck pheasant or blue pheasant
same like a chicken or like my rabbit, Clyde.

Bernie, he stuff Clyde when he die last Easter,
but when I seen my rabbit—
all matted his fur was
and his eyes no was the same;
his teeth was real buck not like the real Clyde.
I say, *Thanks, Bernie.* I know
he trying for be kind to me
but I cry all the way home.
That's why Bernie say he going quit stuffing pets.

One time, Bernie stuffing a pueo.
Bernie he have a phone call
so he tell me sit on his taxidermy stool
and watch so the pueo don't fly away.
I touch the feathers, brown and soft.
I pick up the head but it fall backwards
even if I hold the neck.
The pueo eye all gray
like loose skin and sunken in.
I put my fingers on the eye and make um open
but no more nothing there. Nothing.
Just one dark, black hole.

When Bernie come back,
he put the excelsior body in,

the wires in the claws part and he tell me,
Like put the glass eye in the bird eye socket?
First I make like, *Nah, nah, I no like.*
Then I think about the pueo
and his big, black nothing
under the smooth eye skin.
I pick up the yellow glass eye
with Bernie long tweezer and put um in
the soft clay Bernie put in the bird eye.
And I move the eye until I know
the pueo looking straight at me.

Bernie smooth the feathers down
and put string around the bird.
Why gotta tie um up? I ask him.
Bumbye he like visit you
when you sleeping, he tell.
And he run away from my shop.
You wen' make him see, ass why.
That's why he looking at you.
He gotta rememba your face.

I wait every night
for the pueo come to me.
I look from the picture window
in my living room for the pueo big wings,
his big, yellow glass eye
looking for me.

Turtles

On the wall in Bernard's Taxidermy Shop
is two big, green turtles. They all shiny.
Bernie, he use varnish make um look wet.
Bernie say, before could catch turtles
for the shell or for meat, but now,
he say not suppose to catch turtles
or else the police going arrest you.
He say, when you catch a turtle,
the turtle he cry a tear
from his big, wet eye.
Bernie seen um when he went fish
down South Point side.

He ask if I ever taste turtle meat.
He say, *Ono you know.*
I tell my wife cook
the frozen turtle meat one night
and you come over try some.
Ask your mama first.
I thinking about the tear from the turtle eye.
I tell Bernie I no like.

Bernie say the turtle eggs
look like ping pong balls.
He tell me, his friend Melvin,
the lifeguard down Punalu'u beach,
seen turtle fin marks in the sand
couple weeks ago so him and Bernie
wen' put all the eggs in one hole
and wen' put one cage over so nobody vandal um.

Late one Saturday afternoon,
I was at Bernie's shop helping him sweep up
the loose feathers, this white chemicals,
and sheep wool off the floor,
the phone wen' ring and was Melvin.
Bernie stay all panic on the phone.
Okay, okay. I going close the shop.
C'mon, he tell me. *No need sweep.*
C'mon, c'mon. The turtles hatching.
We neva going see this in our whole life again.
Us get in the Jeep and drive fast down Punalu'u.
No speed, Bernie, I tell him,
bumbye Officer Gomes give you one ticket.
But Bernie, he no listen.

When us get there, close to night time.
Get Melvin and his girlfriend, Teruko.
Bernie's wife stay too—
she work the lei stand down the beach.
The little turtle babies,
they pop their head
right out the black sand.
They all black too.
And when one 'nother one about to come up,
the sand cave in little bit
around the turtle head.
Turtles, they know by instinct
where is the ocean, Bernie tell. *Watch.*
And he turn one baby turtle backwards to the mountain.
Then the turtle he turn
his own self around
and run to the water.

Get plenny. They all running to the water.
They shine when the wave hit them.
And their heads stay bob up

and down in the ocean.
Plenny little heads.
Bernie pick one up and give um to me.
Like take um home?
Take um, take um, he tell me.
I think about the turtles on Bernie wall.
They look like they crying too.
Nah, I tell him.   *I no like um.*
I take the baby turtle to the water edge,
his eye all glassy, his whole body shine,
and I put um down.
No cry now, I tell um,
No cry.

Kid

Bernie and Melvin went up Mauna Kea
couple weeks ago for hunt goat.
They was going make smoke meat
for Melvin's bradda's grad party.
Bernie say they was going over this small lava hill
when they wen' spark one big herd.
But end up Bernie wen' shoot one lady goat
and when he went up near her,
had one small baby goat
crying where the madda was dead.
Bernie say the baby no mo than few days old.

So he bring um back to the shop with him.
Bumbye the baby ma-ke die dead,
no mo mommy, no can eat grass yet.
Bernie give the baby to me.
He buy one whole case of the small
Carnation milks and one baby bottle.
Then he show me how make
half and a half Carnation milk with warm water.
Then how for test um if too hot on my arm.
Bernie say no can be Carnation powder milk
or else the goat get biri-biri.

Bernie put one old blanket on the floor
of the shop and the baby goat,
she sit on my lap when I feed her.
She attack the bottle and by the side of her mouth
get milk bubbles. She kick her legs when she eat
and she make funny kine sounds,
but I smell her neck and kiss her all over.
Goats get a real goat smell.

I smell the sheeps before in Bernie's shop
but they no smell like my goat.
I tell Bernie I call the baby, Lambie.
He say baby goats ain't called lambs.
They call um *kids*.
Baby sheeps is lambs.
I tell him I no care.
She is one lamb to me.

In the morning, I rush to the shop
so I can feed Lambie. When I go school,
I smell like one goat.
Lunch time, I use my home lunch pass
but I no go home.
I go the shop feed Lambie.
Bernie, he make me tuna sandwich or grill cheese
and I eat um on my way back to school.
After school, I run over there
and Lambie, she see me coming
and she wag her tail like one dog
and she prance sideways on all four hoofs.
She knock over Bernie's tools, his knifes,
and some newspapers. Bernie say pretty soon,
I have to take her home and tie her
in the backyard so she can eat grass.
Plus, he say, he tired of sweeping up
goat Raisinets from his floor.

So Bernie and me take Lambie my house in the Jeep.
He get one big oil drum, hollow out,
for Lambie sleep inside.
Bernie say gotta move her around the yard
every week and he show me how.
My madda, she hate Lambie.
She think I nuts stay out there
with my goat till 8:00 at night.

She yelling from the window,
Get in this fricken house.
You think you one goat or what?
Then she tell me if she step on one goat shit
when she hanging laundry, I going get lickens
so I no put Lambie by the clothesline.

Now Bernie say he not going give me
no mo pets 'cause I ditch him.
He say I no visit his shop,
I no sweep for him no mo,
and no mo nobody for talk story with.
I go home and I feel bad
but I come happy when I see Lambie.
But what I seen that day,
I no could believe.
Lambie had eat all my madda's
wild violet hedges by the washing machine
and my madda wen' rake up
all the goat shit in one big pile
next to the hedges.

My madda no even come outside when she yell,
You and your old man friend, Bernie,
better do something about that fricken goat
or I going give um to the old men
across the street and they going eat um.
Stay fuckin' stinkin' up my whole yard.
Get rid of um. Now.

Bernie say we cannot take Lambie
back to the mountains 'cause she too tame.
She no can survive already.
He say his backyard too many of his hunting dogs
so Bernie, he call his friend
at the Onekahakaha Zoo in Hilo.
The man tell we can take Lambie live over there.

KID

Long, the ride to Hilo.
Lambie, she know something wrong.
When we take her in the zoo,
all the peoples watch 'cause she follow me
like one dog on a leash.
The zoo man, he lead Lambie into the big goat cage.
Bernie say the goat cage look exactly
like the place he find Lambie
but I know he trying for make me feel better.
Then he treat me ice shave
from the truck but I no can take even one bite.
I hold um by my lips all cold
when I look at the cage.

The big billies, they surround Lambie.
She looking around for run away.
Then she see me. She cry one cry
I neva going forget in my whole life.
One big, long bleat.
She run over the lava rock hill
close to the side of the cage I stay by.
The billies all follow her.
They smell the human hands on her.
They smell her all over.
She back up against the fence.
Leave her alone, I tell.
Bernie, help her.
She, she just one kid.

Glass

Bernie he everytime show off his glass floaters.
I wen' tell him I like one
but he say, *Not the same somebody give you.*
Mo betta you find um yourself.
Go ask your mama if you can go Kaaluwalu
with me this Sunday.
That's where all the glass balls stay,
but hard for fine.
Sometimes you think you see one
but ass only broken glass.

My madda make me do all kine work
before I can go. She say, *Tell that old man*
I like you home by 5:00
or I calling the cops.
Who he think him, your fadda?
We no need his pity.
I no think I going tell Bernie all that.
I take the tuna musubi I made for me and him
and walk to the taxidermy shop.

I real early so I put on
the old hunting boots Bernie gave me
the time us went hunting for pheasants.
Was little too big so I wen' stuff
some toilet paper in the toes part.
Pretty soon Bernie come.

Kinda early, eh? he tell
and he adjust the visor on his head.
Bernie kinda bald.
How come? Your mama yell at you again?
I no say nothing.

Us get in the Jeep and pass the cow pasture
by the just burn sugar cane field.
Then us pass Punalu'u and Honoapu Mill.
Bernie go slow through Naalehu
then Waiohinu by the Mark Twain monkeypod tree.
Bernie tell me stories about every stone wall,
every old graveyard, every stream,
and even the monkeypod tree.

When us get to Kaaluwalu,
Bernie give me my Calrose rice bag
and help me tie um around my waist.
He tell, *Anything look pretty good to you*
like I can use um for mount something,
pick um up, eh? Driftwood especially.
He help me put my knapsack on.
And no get your hopes up, okay? he tell.
Not every time get glass balls.
Maybe one in five trips I find one.

Get plenny bagasse on the beach.
Get plastic floaters all over.
All kine broken nylon net
and plenny broken glass
from the glass balls that never make it to shore.
Shine like green and blue stones in the water.

Then way by the top of the shoreline,
I see one nub part of the glass ball
so I tell Bernie I going check um out.
I dig in the bagasse and right there
in the wet cane rubbish is one small glass ball,
light blue and cool in the shade of the naupaka bushes.
I hold um gentle in my hands.
I no can even see my fingers.
I see the clouds, the sky moving.
I see my eyes.

FOUR

My Eyes Adore You

Aunty Nancy have a baby boy; he no mo daddy.
Us had one before, but now, he don't know us.
Aunty Nancy's Baby Boy have sev-ral choice for daddy.
She waiting to see who he look like
when he grow up.

Mama stand by her bedroom door and push
the pink and red bamboo beads aside. She blast
the musk oil on each inside thigh.
Shit. I hate kids.

Tonight got the 39 and Under
basketball league at the high school gym.
All Mama's and Aunty Nancy *classmates* playing in this league.
That's what they told us.
But we know

that over there's
the right place to be for finding men.
And talking after the games.
A   long   time in the parking lot. And beers.

Me and my sista, C, going be walking
home by ourself tonight.
Maybe me by myself. C sometimes stay with Mama.
I going be carrying Baby Boy home. Again.

The gym lights look gold.

I hear squeaking of gym shoes on hardwood floor
and feet pounding up and down the court. Men yelling.
I smell wet towels under hot lights and sweaty shoes.
I smell Mama and Aunty Nancy, Jovan Musk oil yelling.

WillyJoe playing this game.
The Fil-Ams versus the Weekend Warriors.
Somebody's arm hit WillyJoe when he see us coming.

Mama to Aunty Nancy:

Not bad, Willy.
I mean for this town
and what we get
for choose from.
But he neva did grad.
He supposed to be same class
with my cousin Frankie.

Check him,
check him,
surfa body and ehu hair.
But he kinda talk simple-minded stuff.
Maybe I might want to do him
  (whispering low now so I cannot hear)
every night, 'cause you know, Nance,
you take what goods
you get in this fuckin' town,
and his grapes, they hanging
pretty heavy on the vine.
I take anybody's grapes in my mouth
for drink some wine.

Baby Boy crying so Aunty Nancy flicks his mouth.
See you guys later, I tell them.
I going sit outside on the steps.
Mama could care less by this time.
I see it in her glistening eyes.

Uncle Reggie, the Parks and Rec man, eating pun-kin
seeds outside the door under the bulb
light swinging in the squeaky wind.
He flicking the shells in the big tin trash can
'cause he the one in charge.

He give me orange Fanta, one handful of pun-kin seeds.
The scoreboard horn go off. End of game.
The men go into the locker room.
The men in the next game come running out onto
the court high school basketball team style
with a layup drill and jumpshots.

Then Uncle Reggie say to me,

> *I wen' ask Willy for take you home tonight*
> *so you no need walk home Baby Boy by yourself.*
> *I no like you walking home like that. Not safe.*

> *Me, I gotta clean the concession, check the locker rooms,*
> *dust mop the floors then lock up the gym*
> *afta the last game so going be too late*

> *for me take you home by the time I pau all that.*
> *And I tell you what else, if Nancy come out here*
> *before Willy pau shower, leave that baby with her.*

> *Ass hers. Not yours. There.*
> *There WillyJoe.*

Willy hair all slick back.
Willy smell like Aqua Velva.
No. Like Brut.
No. Like musk oil.

C'mon. Us go, WillyJoe says. *No walk by yourself.*
Your madda going be here with all the boys
till three o'clock drinking beer.
Her and Nancy. Us go.

The yellow Datsun smell like ripe
strawberry and the seats fuzzy. The back seat down
and Willy put one tape in the 8-track.

> *(though I never laid a hand on you)*
> *My eye adore you.*
> *Like a million mile away from me* (he singing soft)
> *you couldn't see how I adore you,*
> *so close,*
> *so close and yet so far.*
> (he singing to me, I think)

He catch himself and he come shame.
We go play um loud. Real loud
the way I like um, he says. *You like go*
straight home or you like go riding first?
Us go riding. I like show you someting nice.

I so stun by his face.
The smell.
What he saying.
How he sing to me.
I cannot talk.

He park behind the baseball field, the back side.
He tell me the story of green
he made up from what the field look like when all lit up
'cause he the P and R scoreboard man for Uncle Reggie.

How seagreen and aquamarine almost the same.
How he watch me
sitting in the stands
waiting for Uncle Reggie.

And a pheasant, a Japanese blue ringneck, he seen
in the middle of the baseball field early one morning.
How his Uncle Penny told him about its intro-duck-tion
to the island. And how on the morning

him and Uncle Reggie seen um,
the bird yank his red face up and down and straight up
when he catch the downwind smell of a man
and fly away all jerky into the sky.

He tell me if he was a goat
how he would love to eat
the manienie, honohono and dandelions on the hill
next to the field 'cause look so lush from here.

How he watch me
swimming laps after school,
walking home close to night,
how my eyes
just like his, he say:

    Need somebody to read um right for once
    'cause they brown and chilly, scare
    sometimes, just like his, he say.

       though I never lay a hand on you

He changing the end of the song,
making up the words.

My eyes.
My eyes. Fill.
He ain't simple, Mama. Ain't
simple.
Ain't.

Ravine

Mama by the ravine picking wild
squash shoots off
of the em-bankment of the dry stream.
The sun, all steep light, sharp on my back.
I sitting on the guard rail above the ravine.

Watching the cane green hands dancing.
Down in the stream,
only big boulders and swamp smelling pools of mosquito water
with algae and air
bubbles caught like frog eggs.
And heat rising up in wavy vapors.

I thinking maybe a flash
flood come and take my Mama away (for little while)
down a raging brown river, down
into the choppy ocean.
And dump her there.
(Wish.)

So I listen hard for a rumble upstream.
Gimme the rice bag, Lucy.
Whatchu doing daydreaming up there?
Get your ass down here right now. Now.

She mad 'cause maybe the Filipino
ladies from church see her picking squash shoots
like we all poor, and she no like um think
we worse off than them.

I go down the em-bankment slow
so I no slide into the rocks.
Mama already snatching the rice bag
out of my hands and make me do a little slide.

I slip down on my ass
and grab onto a small guava tree branch.
She lucky I come with her. She beg me (all nice)
after I come home from school
to walk with her to the stream.

We going up there 'cause we ain't got nothing
to eat, that she going fry the squash shoots she pick
with frozen bacon. And if we real lucky,
Mama going find squash all ready to pick.
The squash she fry with frozen pork belly.
Cook us some hot rice tonight.

I sitting on the em-bankment now.
I feel all red inside below my heart
when I think about WillyJoe last night
and all the warm breath I felt so close to my hearing.

WillyJoe WillyJoe WillyJoe.

I see Mama's eyes flash
toward the road checking out for old ladies.
She so para-noid.
I picking some dirt out of my fingernail and killing
ants that I lure on my finger.
I watch them sniff me a little
and take a few steps, before I cut
off their heads with my fingernail.

And then it comes.

Spell For Triple Luck:

Sunlight through the bottom
of a mayonnaise jar
you find in the ravine;

hold it close to your eyelid
until the cool of the glass go away;
spin the bottle seven times slow.

Rub maroon velvet cloth
you steal from the Methodist church
on your lips. Whisper
soft three times,

He loves me.
He loves me not.
He loves me.

I look up all of a sudden.
And I see the yellow Datsun coming up the cane dirt road.
Somebody
glinting a mirror at me;
my eye catch a sliver of sunlight.

Someone on the passenger side.
And the 8-track tape real loud.

Keep on rolling,
Mississippi moon
won't cha keep on shining on me.

I see my sista leaning over and steering
the car and tooting the horn and laughing.
Mama's head poke up from the wild squash vines.

She yelling at me,
Who the fuck's tooting their goddamn horn at me, Lucy?
C, Mama. I yelling back.
Who? Fuck Lucy, speak up, shit.
C, Mama, C.
Who she with?

She, she with.
I see them,

but I cannot believe that WillyJoe
would be with my sista.
Not after what he said
and what he did last night.
Me and WillyJoe.
By the field.
No.

Words stuck inside my throat.
She, she with WillyJoe, I scream.
In the yellow Datsun.

She shining the mirror at me and laughing
as I shield my eyes.

    (Shine, Lucy, SHINE.)
    You the star of the song.
    Glint slivers of sun,
    light spark in your eye.

Willy take the mirror from her.
She laughing so hard, the whole car shaking.
Willy hanging his arm out of the window.
He smoking Kool Milds, no shirt on.
He put it on the bucket seat like all the men do,
the seat wearing a shirt.

C motion for us to come over.
Leaning over Willy. Take a drag off of his cigrette.
Mama lean over Willy window.
She press her breasts
together to look like she got more.

I lean on the front of the car.
Casting another spell.
C yelling over the 8-track tape.

Get in, Mama. Willy was cruising by
Cosmo Meat Market when he seen me
by Country Mart buying slush.
So I told him I neva know where you was,
so if he could help me find you.

Mama squirming like she trying
to get her breast even *more* uplift
while nodding her head sweetly.
And Willy (oh he so swweeeet), my sista continue,
he say he want *to help me.*

Thanks, eh, thank you so much, WillyJoe,
says my Mama all perfeck English,
'cause Lucy and me, we would've have to walk home
in the pitch dark. (C'mon, Lucy.)
She grit her teeth and say this.

Willy looking at my eyes
but I don't dare meet his
for very long.
Nobody can know,

he sing to me,
he in my ear,
he watch me.
All the time.

He darting at Mama, her face in his window,
her breasts all squeeze up,
and C leaning over him, her hand on his thigh.
He looking left and right, left and right.
At me. Poor WillyJoe.

Mama run over to the front passenger seat
where C sitting and she yell, *Get out of there, C.*
Let your mother sit up front.

RAVINE

You kids *in the back.*
She says this low through biting teeth.
Get-in-the-back-with-Lucy.

But C, she just scoot over.
She sitting on the hand brake between the two bucket seats.
Lickens when we get home.
Spread her legs to accom-mo-date for the gear shift.
Double lickens with the orange Hot Wheels tracks.

I know she hoping and praying that Willy gotta put
his gear into reverse; *it* being right *there,*
right-into-her—*Gunfunnit, Lucy,* Mama screaming.
Get into the car. Willy busy, you know.
And I slide into the back seat.

Mama throw the rice bag full
of squash shoots by my feet.
Mama, C and the Doo-bees all competing for Willy.
I looking at my dirty hands.

>   *like a lazy flowing river,*
>   *surrounding castles in the sky-eye,*
>   *the clouds are growing bigger.*

Shift into second
and my sista squirm
and straighten her back, throw
her head back like Mama and roll her eyes.
Willy move his hand away fast.
Back on the wheel.
Shift reluctant into third. (Giggle.)
Then fourth. (Ummm.)

Willy adjust the rear view mirror til he see my eyes.
And I see his eyes.
He smile at me.

---

oh blackwater, keep on rolling

His eye on me in the rear view mirror.
A smile waiting for me to answer,
his eyes looking me over, up.
Up and down, roll on over me.

The pheasant, Lucy. The blue pheasant.
WillyJoe talking, and all the noise stop.
My Mama's mouth.
C not screaming.
The 8-track turn down.
They all want to hear what WillyJoe saying.

I seen him again. On the field this morning.
Right where was the odda time.
His eyes right in mine, promise kine.
We was staring at each odda long time.
He get red eyes.

Ask your Uncle Reggie. Us was fertilizing, me and him.
You rememba what I told you last night
when us went up the field and was talking
and playing tapes and.

Willy catch himself talking too much.
Nobody say nothing for a long time.
I smile at him.
The car stop.

I the first one out of the car outside our house.
I take the rice bag full of wild squash shoots.
Mama run to Willy's window.
C still on the hand brake.

WillyJoe catch the downwind smell
and want to fly too,
his head going left and right,
left and right.

Empty Heart

i.

He lay me down on the straw
in the shed behind his papa's house, listen
for a while to the cane trucks passing
on the plantation dirt road, the lychee tree crackly

leaves in the early night time;
chickens clucking low, low.
He touch my forehead with his long fingers, crawl them
across my face like little feet.

He turn on the Eveready.
On his fingers as they track across my face.
On my chin where he draw light finger circles. Down my neck,
light shining, following a finger slide

down my neck, and fingers light around each tit-ty.
Spotlight left. He smile, weak-like.
Spotlight right, his breathing rapid.
His finger in my belly button, swirl it

around and around, eyes rolling, slow,
flashlight fall, go off by itself.

    I know what else he want to touch.

    Crawl slow,
    slow there
    then stop
    in his finger tracks.

He pretend like was one accident he touch me here and here,
his fingers into there and there. Stop.
Take a fat red crayola he find
in the corner of the shed and draw pictures in the asphalt

right outside the door, wind pouring into us now, erasing
our breath in the window-less shed.
He say it will melt in the slope of the sun,
stay there forever. Then he says,

> *Write your name and mine,*
> *long and curvy.*

But I draw a school girl shampooing her hair with Prell
in a tub full of bath oil beads.
Then I draw my name next to his:
on the sidewalk in red, red crayola.

Empty heart

Empty heart lov WillyJo

ii.

He not in school anymore but he drive
his yellow Datsun to the parking lot by the baseball field,
sneak across Alto's yard behind the school fence

and hide on the slope full of dandelions and puffballs.
He wait by the fence until the bell for recess time.
I run to him fast and sneaky as I can, hide

behind the hibiscus hedge, sit in the tall ironweed.
I put my fingers through the chain links to touch his face.
He kiss my fingers.

WillyJoe pass me cut persimmons so I can think in school.
But I can eat um if, only if, I let him feed me.
Then he sit there and teach me about places
he think he seen. Words he learn from Uncle Penny:

> *Bangkok, a beach with waves like blacksands.*
> *Or maybe he dream it,*
> *Madrid, the lights all blue and yellow cities curling,*
> places where he drank sunrise with mini pink umbrellas.

> *The redpurple vein croton, varicose green leaf.*
> *The story of the mouflon sheep, not native,*
> *tie-up in Felix yard.*
> *The making of a Pontiac.*
> *Beef cuts at Cosmo's like sir-loin tip.*

> *Yellow lights and fingers through the chain link.*

More. Tell me. More.
Tell me. And he tell me about

            bells ringing,

the bell ringing, and the teacher yelling,
Get away from her before I call the cops, you
mo-lester. Help, help somebody help me.

Trespasser! Quick, get the principal.
This child mo-lester's been after this
girl for a long time.

Scram, you big good-for-nothing
before the cops get here.
The teacher grabbing my arm and pulling me away.

Scratch my arm on the hibiscus branch.
My arm bleeding.
Willy's fingers hanging on to the chain link fence,

his face, his lips withering.
And animal screams from his mouth
like the sound I heard his bunnies make when the mama rabbit

step on them in the middle of the night.
We was sleeping next to his papa's shed.

iii.

Willy know plenny words
he learn from his Uncle Penny
who teach him on Saturdays on the porch of his house.
Willy bring the Planters cocktail peanuts and six-pack Primo.

He learn all his words.
And the drunker they get, out come the tequila, Cuer-vo,
fresh pick pretend lime (from the kumquat tree),
and the rock salt.

Then Uncle Penny is Perfeser Penny.

> A clot is a co-agu-late of blood.
> Paprika is a red sneeze, good for the artery.
> And de-creshando coming down from adrena-lin.

Willy is himself.

> Tell me about coitus.

Willy tell me come learn and I
can be myself
too.

iv.

He the cherub. Come from St. Joseph's
pink church on the corner across from Cosmo Meat Market,
the post office, and the one bank in town.
The pink church surrounded by jacaranda trees

and African tulip trees. Get orange and purple petals
on the gravestones the priest sweep every day.
One day, Willy say he going read me
the names on the stones

before the petal juice and black fungus fill
the grooves and the names all gone.
And one day he say he going ring
the church bell for me.

One day.

>   *I going cure the blood clot
>   in your emp-ty heart.*

v.

By the saltwater ponds.
Near the black sand beach.

Late afternoon.
Salt mist all around, the ocean
rough and choppy today.
A big hill of sea grass in front of the car,

and Willy singing,

>   *Some-where ov-a the rain-bow,*

a capella, he singing,

>   *Good-bye yellow brick road,*

about his fuu-chur it

>   *lie be-yond the yellow brick road.*

EMPTY HEART

He play a tape of Elton John.
Like sound-track in a movie,

like background music
that perfectly match what the actors doing.

Like today.

But Willy, he say he have no brain.
He say he stupid, he a dropout
with so-sho and emo-sho handicap.

Willy say before in his special class
they dig weeds for the ag teacher all day
so he can be

  the Scarecrow long and soft.

Me, he say, I the star of the song.
Humming low and holding my fingers in his fingers.

  I Judy Gar-land.
  I Dor-ty.

And my breath he say, smell like paprika.

He WillyJoe, the Big Scarecrow, scared
scared of a lot of things.
Scared of me.

Scared of my body.
Maybe one day I no let him touch me anymore.
Anywhere. Over there.

No fingers crawling no more.
Scared of my nostrils flaring.
So scared of me.

ScarecrowJoe.

vi.

One day
I going write
about you,
I tell him.

Sitting under the tree in the schoolyard,
the light from the softball game make the whole school

turn to day. WillyJoe the scoreboard man
but he tell my Uncle Reggie that he get one date tonight.

Uncle Reggie tell Willy got the night off.
Willy hanging from the jungle gym and make me

sit at the very top.
Right over his face.

No moonlight.
His fingers gripping the bars and his legs too long,

bent at the knees.
Him sniffling and smiling.

In the grass, rolling together
and laughing in the school yard,

making stepped on rabbit sounds until it echo
in the school buildings, throwing glass

and tinkling sounds.
And licking each other's eyelids.

vii.

One day,
I going write
about you
walking down the road,

bouncing the cane truck inner tube
on the hot asphalt
right over the place
where we wrote

in red,

Empty heart.

    WillyJo lov Dor-ty.

Name Me Is

WillyJoe is a name
on a tree   next to mine.

He ask me to scratch it
in the curve of the branch

with the soda tab
he not using for the soda tab neck-

lace for next year's
Christmas tree, so I digging

and digging his name deep
into the tree until we scar

the branch all orange,
our names, bright orange scratch sap.

> *If I was blind, I could still smell you, you know. 'Cause you always smell good to me. Like maybe Prell shampoo on your hair and Camay soap on your body and I know for sure you put Mums deodorant, the creme kine on your underarm.*

> *Or I could hear you, you know. Like right now if I close my eyes, I can hear you scratching and scratching on that tree branch all by yourself. Or I could hear you whistling our secret whistle, three times, from way down the street. The way I call you out your bedroom window at night.*

> *And if I was blind, I could still taste you down where you let me taste you, where I leave one big silva dolla size red mark. Yeah, I tink I know you good. So if God like know, I tink I could be blind. (And not mine too much.)*

A name on my folder
in fat black marker

(but nobody can know)

so I write like Willy write
when he feeling proud of himself,
M L   LuvS   M E F

Mrs. Livingston loves Mr. Eddie's Father.
I hide it with my arm

when my Mama look at me;
I write on the school bathroom wall

and the next day, watch the janitor
paint us away.

>   *Real lovers. Real lovers no sweat, you know. And afta,*
> *real lovers smoke one cigrette. Real lovers, they shut their*
> *eyes, roll um back in the socket and throw their head back. Then*
> *their mouth fall open. The girl, she wearing red lipstick.*
> *Gotta be red. But no tongues when they kiss.*
>   *Real lovers, the man, he carry the girl to the bed. She*
> *wearing pink with pink feathers kine robe. He throw her down*
> *on the bed, you know. She bounce then sink like the thing real*
> *soft. The music fade in soft first, then cree-shan-do until the*
> *screen get all cloudy. Then dee-cree-shan-do.*
>   *I love you Mrs. Livingston. Then you say,* I love you,
> Mr. Eddie's father. *Nobody going know, see? For real, nobody*
> *can know 'cause Mrs. Livingston, she in her true heart love*
> *Mr. Eddie's father. And Mr. Eddie's father in his true heart love*
> *Mrs. Livingston. But they neva let nobody know.*
>   *I could feel um. You couldn't feel um? The way they look*
> *and the way they turn their heads for see each other? But you*
> *know what? Nobody wen' really know.*

Willy ask me write our names
in the black sand

and he run find a bamboo stick
so I can write cursive
the way he like
again and again:

WillyJoe —*n*— Me
M L —*n*— M E F
LoVe LoVeS *LuvS*
wj —*n*— L

Over and over
until our names all smooth away.

You know the shell bracelet I wen' make for you? I wen'
pick each shell so could be one surprise. I wen' choose only the
lavender ones, and I saving all the browns and pinks.
    Then I wen' size um all in one row, small to big (like
Uncle Penny tell me) til they all even. And I sit on the porch
with him last Saturday and string um slow 'cause Uncle Penny
tell I can learn the power is the Word.
    'Cause each shell Uncle made um one word. For power.
Like magic charm. I wen' start with
    oral-ly. (send it by mouth)
    Then petroglyph. (the name of one picture)
    Infinity. (mean for-eva)
    I know the word I give for each shell on this whole
bracelet 'cause I wen' name um all for you. Each one. And the
last one is you, Lucy. Lavender.

My name on a matchbook
in his lumberjacket pocket,

he had um in his hand,
all night in the movie.

I have a matchbook too
with his name on it,

WillyJoe WillyJoe WillyJoe

but my math teacher grabs it
from me and reads it.

Where you got this idiot's
jacket? I'm gonna call your mama tonight.

He so mean. He says I love a idiot.
What's wrong with me? Wrong,

wrong with the love
I write on a matchbook.

Was pale thin blue. The Lucy on the palm of my hand
'cause I know you like I know the palm of my hand. Get it,
Lucy? Was India ink with one reg-la needle and string. I wen'
copy your name cursive like how you wen' write um for me on
the matches.
I wish you could wake up in the morning and walk with me
up the stream, way   way up the mountain, the place I go by
myself. And watch me cross the long wooden bridge and no sked
for fall. I dive into the water, all clear like aquablue, you know,
Lucy. Clear. You eva seen clear blue?
Gotta be na-ked or no can go with me to the stream 'cause
I bafe there (without soap), my whole body smelling like one
river, and when I look under the water with my eyes open, no
so-wa, you know, and I going see you, clear as I see you now. I
going see you. All. Feel so clean. Smell real good like one
real man, you know.

Then afta, us can rest on the big boulders by the side and
talk if us like live ova there for the rest of our life. Build
us one tree house with three stories so that the wild pig cannot
hurt us, Lucy. You can make banana pancake for breakfast,
and I can catch prawn for dinna like one real family, you and
me, Lucy, and all our baby up in the tree house.

I too stupid for you, WillyJoe tell me.
(But he not crying.)
Teach me to write.

Teach me so I can write
your name, he say, with the sparklers

on New Years the way I cursive
his name with sparkler

light all orangegreen
and smoke, a line of green,

it stay in the nightblack,
light for awhile.

   Do it again. (He clapping for me)
   Again.

Me and WillyJoe celebrating
New Years by the school building,

burning our sparklers
and at 12 o'clock, he kiss

my ear. WillyJoe and me,
Happy New Year.

NAME ME IS

I stay singing to you, Lucy — in — the — sky-eye —
with — diamonds. Kissing you there.

    The nightclouds stay evaporate, until the black so
faraway. You eva seen one night unreal like Christmas time? Or
maybe one night, like you was up Mauna Loa, and everyting
seem so pull away from the ground so get more space between us
and the sky.

    LucyLucyLucyLucyLucyLucyLucyLucy—Loo—saaaay. We
stay in the sky tonight. My hand belong here. You going let me
leave um? I like feel you. 'Cause one day going have more than
one hand. Promise.

He take my shirt off that night, then his,
and lay face down across my lap.

I touch his shoulder blades, light
fingers first. They broad and brownsmooth,
feeling good, good, see

him shiver when I heat
the sparkler tip red
and ribbon it in the black night,

(He know what I want to do)

bring it down on his skin, burn
the first line.

It smell like herbs in the kitchen bottles,
the skin soft crackling like that and Willy,
he flinch at first,

then he thaw out heavy on my lap
so I heat the tip of the sparkler again
and burn his name on his back:

137

W
WIL-LY (You wrote Willy)
Sounding out the word
like I do in school.
JOE   (Now says WillyJoe)

And he lick the crack
in my folded leg,
with every burn line I make,
licking up his tears from me,

and I smell his blood, taste um,
taste just like rust.

Now, he say, *Your name on your back,*
and I lie face down across his lap.

I hear the match strike and flame,
then I feel him burn me long,
and my body squeeze first,

then release the color gray,
that fall to my feet in slow motion,
gray waves out of my eyes,
in and out with the sweet smell
of skin burning.

No crying, now, Willy says,
but I taste the tears:
he writing best he can.

(As far as he know)
(As far as I teach him)

burning the main con-so-nans
of my name hard

into my back meat:

    L U Sounding out the word.
    C (See.)   A deep, deep curve.

Sounding out the word
like I do in school
again and again.

I feeling all thaw out
in my bones, all melting
from what he done,

so he light a sparkler
and tell me write my name
in the black night,

and when the sparkler all done,
we both withering
in all the skin smell and blood,
lying on our stomachs

in the grass, WillyJoe and Me,
we no dare touch the scars
on our backs, too wet
to put our shirts on
'cause the skin might stick,

so sitting there,
swabbing each other's tears.

    Look what we done.

We walk over to the tree
and look at our names carve
for infinity.

Look, he says.
This proof for-eva and eva.

I IS, he says.
YOU IS too.

He turn around.

Look at my back, Lucy.
I IS here too.

I touch him.

WILLYJOE, he says,
For-eva, right there.

I IS too,
I say soft.
I no like WillyJoe hear me.

I feel the thick, clear liquid
move slow out of my name
on my back, touch it

with my own fingers, feel
my name on my back

all the way inside.

I IS.
Ain't *nobody*
tell me
otherwise.

About the Author

PHOTO BY KEELY LUKE

Lois-Ann Yamanaka
was born in Ho'olehua, Molokai,
then raised in Hilo, Ka'u, and Kona.
She lives in Kahalu'u.